Dear Mr Morpingo

*Inside the World of
Michael Morpurgo*

Geoff Fox

Illustrations by Michael Foreman

Wizard Books

Published in the UK in 2004 by Wizard Books Ltd.,
an imprint of Icon Books Ltd., The Old Dairy,
Brook Road, Thriplow,
Cambridge SG8 7RG
email: wizard@iconbooks.co.uk
www.iconbooks.co.uk/wizard

Sold in the UK, Europe, South Africa
and Asia by Faber and Faber Ltd.,
3 Queen Square, London WC1N 3AU
or their agents

Distributed in the UK, Europe, South Africa
and Asia by TBS Ltd., Frating Distribution Centre,
Colchester Road, Frating Green, Colchester CO7 7DW

Published in Australia in 2004
by Allen & Unwin Pty. Ltd.,
PO Box 8500, 83 Alexander Street,
Crows Nest, NSW 2065

Distributed in Canada by
Penguin Books Canada,
10 Alcorn Avenue, Suite 300,
Toronto, Ontario M4V 3B2

ISBN 1 84046 607 3

Typesetting by Hands Fotoset

Printed and bound in the UK by Clays of Bungay

For Pam

Contents

CONTENTS

Photographs

PHOTOGRAPHS

Illustrations

[All illustrations reproduced by kind permission of Michael Foreman.]

How Nothing
Nearly Happened

How Nothing
Nearly Happened

It was 1944 and the Second World War was still raging. Hitler's doodlebugs – rocket-propelled bombs like small planes with no pilots – were dropping out of the sky over southern England. For safety's sake, the infant Michael Morpurgo – though he wasn't called Morpurgo then – and his older brother Peter had been taken by their mother away from the London area to stay with a distant relation up North.

This relation was a vicar, so Michael, Peter and his mother shared the rectory with the vicar's family. It was raining, but Michael's mother firmly believed that all babies needed fresh air, every day, rain or shine. She wrapped little Michael up warm, snuggled him down in his pram and parked him safely at the back of the garage out of sight behind the vicar's car. Michael was sleeping peacefully when the vicar came out, jumped in his car and drove off. That would have been fine except, somehow, Michael's pram had got hooked onto the back bumper. Michael and the pram went jolting faster and faster down the drive behind the accelerating car.

Luckily, the pram couldn't keep pace with the car and it came adrift, tipping Michael out onto the drive. He had a few bruises – but he was alive. But if the pram had *not* come adrift, if the vicar with the pram still hooked on behind had got as far as a busy main road, if Michael had landed on the sharp stones of a rockery, he would never have been able to write his books or to read and tell and talk about stories to audiences all over Britain as the Children's Laureate. And thousands of children from city primary schools would never have been able to spend a week on a farm milking cows, mucking out pigs, digging ditches – and listening to Michael tell his stories.

Nothing nearly happened. It was as close as that.

This exciting start to life seems right for the author of such stories as *War Horse*, *Kensuke's Kingdom* and *Private Peaceful*. However, Michael did not grow up in the way you might expect someone who has written almost 100 books (he's lost count) to grow up. He was lucky as a small child – he had plenty of poems and stories read to him. But as he grew older, he did not read every book he could get his hands on; neither did he fill up exercise books with his own amazing stories while he was still at primary school. There *were* a lot of books around at home, but he didn't like most of them. In fact, he was almost afraid of them. He certainly did not enjoy writing. He was, he says, 'the typical reluctant reader and reluctant writer'. There may have been no computer games to play when he was a boy, but Michael could always find plenty of things to do to avoid reading a book.

It wasn't until he'd left school that Michael came to love reading. And not long after he came to love reading, he discovered, with the help of some children he was teaching, that he also loved telling stories and then, only a little later, writing stories. He has been telling and writing stories ever since.

This book tells Michael's story. It also answers the question every audience asks Michael: 'Where do you get your ideas from?' There is a chapter about how Michael gets started when he is writing a story, how he makes his characters come alive, how he gives them voices and how he keeps you wanting to turn the next page, impatient to find out what happens next – in fact, about how he writes. You'll read about a friendship which changed Michael's life, about the CDs he would take with him if he were stranded on a desert island, about what he'd like to write in the future, about … but that's probably enough to be going on with.

It took Michael many years to discover the person he wanted to be: a storyteller, a writer in close touch with the young readers he writes for, excited by the places he explores and the people he meets on his travels, excited by the journeys he makes in his mind. He and his wife Clare had a long search to make before they found somewhere they felt they belonged, where they could find their roots. When at last they did, Michael says, 'I could be comfortable in my own skin.'

This book begins with that search.

Somewhere to Belong

Beards, Nonsense, Mozart and Uncles

When Michael looks back on his childhood and his early adult life, he feels he never belonged anywhere; he had no roots.

He was born in 1943 in St Alban's in Hertfordshire. After his adventure in the flying pram in Northumberland, Michael and his family returned to Hertfordshire in the summer of 1945 at the end of the war. They lived with his mother's parents at Radlett, about fifteen miles north of London. Michael's father was still serving in the Army in Baghdad and, although the war was over, he was not released from duty for many months.

Grandfather Emile Cammaerts was Belgian and in his youth in Brussels he had been a well-known poet. At the beginning of the First World War, one of his poems became famous as a patriotic rallying call to his countrymen and women, urging them to resist the occupying German Army. The poem was set to music by the English composer Edward Elgar and performed at a concert in London to support Belgian refugees who had fled to England. More than half a century later, Michael read his grandfather's poem, accompanied by Elgar's music, at a concert in Ypres, the site of an important First World War battle in Belgium close to the French border. Michael's grandmother was English, but when she was establishing a reputation as a young opera singer in Europe, Emile Cammaerts had heard her perform. The poet fell for the opera singer, they married and moved to England. Michael's grandfather somehow left the fiery young poet behind in Belgium; he became a

Michael's grandparents, 1964.

very English, tweed-suited gentleman and a professor at London University.

What young Michael liked especially about his grandfather was his flaming red beard. Grandfather was very fond of the Victorian writer Edward Lear. He read his grandson such poems as 'The Owl and the Pussycat' and 'The Dong with the Luminous Nose', but the one Michael enjoyed most as he sat on his grandfather's knee was this limerick:

> There was an Old Man with a beard,
> Who said, 'It is just as I feared! –
>   Two Owls and a Hen,
>   Four Larks and a Wren,
> Have all built their nests in my beard!'

Michael's fingers could not resist reaching up to explore that luxurious red beard, no doubt checking for nests.

Grandmother was not so easy to get to know as Grandfather. Michael felt that even his own mother was a little afraid of her. Not because she was fierce or bad-tempered. Quite the opposite. She was unbelievably *good*; you could never imagine her doing anything wrong. She always wore long, flowing, old-fashioned dresses and, says Michael, 'As her grandson, I thought she was the woman God would have married.'

Michael's mother and his grandmother frequently read poems and stories to the boys. They were wonderful readers, for both were professionally trained stage performers. Even now, when Michael reads Rudyard Kipling's 'The Elephant's Child' or 'The Cat that Walked by Himself' from *Just So Stories*, he can hear the rhythms of his mother's voice. If you read 'The Elephant's Child' aloud, Michael thinks, you can almost *taste* the music and joy of the language:

> Then Kolokolo Bird said, with a mournful cry, 'Go to the banks of the great grey-green, greasy Limpopo River, all set about with fever-trees …'

Since that great grey-green, greasy river flows in and out of the story several times, young Michael joined in with his mother whenever it appeared. He also loved the fun and excitement of the tug-of-war between the Crocodile and the Elephant's Child, whose trunk is being painfully used as the rope. Since Michael's mother was an actress, she was no doubt especially good at the Elephant Child's strangled cry of 'Led go! You are hurtig be!' as his nose, caught in the Crocodile's teeth, is stretched longer and longer.

Then there were the nonsense poems of Lewis Carroll's *Alice's Adventures in Wonderland* and *Alice Through the Looking Glass* to enjoy together. They read

Michael, right, with brother Peter, 1948.

'Jabberwocky' ("Twas brillig and the slithy toves/Did gyre and gimble in the wabe') which Alice finds printed back-to-front in a Looking Glass book. Michael probably thought, as Alice did in the story, 'it seems to fill my head with ideas – only I don't exactly know what they are!' Michael enjoyed the music of the language of the poems and stories. And there always seemed to be music playing on the gramophone at Radlett – frequently Mozart, no doubt the choice of his opera singer grandmother. Michael writes his stories now with music echoing around the house; very often it will be a Mozart CD in the player.

Playing with the rhythm of words became a part of his childhood. It was about this time, his mother later told him, that she overheard him rocking on his bed, chanting to himself, 'Zanzibar! Zanzibar! Marzipan! Zanzibar!' Like most successful authors, Michael never wastes a good memory. Fifty years later, a child chants those same words in his story, *The Wreck of the Zanzibar*.

From his grandparents' house in Radlett, Michael moved in 1946 to live in a flat in Philbeach Gardens, near Earl's Court in south-west London. Some of Michael's aunts were frequent visitors to Radlett and Philbeach Gardens with their young children. Their husbands, like Michael's father, were still away serving in the Armed Forces. Although Michael had never met them, he was also very aware of two uncles who had fought in the war. They were often the subject of conversations between the adults at home. Indeed, he saw his Uncle Peter in his RAF uniform every day, there on the mantelpiece in a silver photograph frame. Peter Cammaerts had been a navigator in a bomber, plotting its route night after night across the North Sea to Germany to drop its deadly load on the weapon factories and cities of the enemy. When his plane was hit by anti-aircraft fire and his pilot killed, Uncle Peter took the controls to keep the aircraft flying while the other members of the crew drifted down to safety in their parachutes. Time ran out for Uncle Peter; he could not escape before the bomber crashed and he died in the wreckage.

Michael did not get to know his other uncle, Francis Cammaerts, until many years after the war, but he did know that Uncle Francis had done something very important, very secret and very dangerous. At the outbreak of war in 1939, Francis had registered as a pacifist, since he did not believe in killing under any circumstances. When his brother Peter had been killed, Francis had decided that he too must now join up for military service. At first, he worked as a medical orderly; but with his Belgian background, Francis spoke perfect French and that was a rare and valuable skill. After training, he was parachuted into France and became a leader with the French Resistance, making life as difficult as possible for the occupying German Army. The men of the Maquis, as the Resistance fighters were called, often lived rough in the forests and caves of the mountains, making quick hit-and-run raids and blowing up railway lines or bridges. They also helped escaping refugees and airmen to avoid capture on their way to neutral Spain.

Years later, Francis' work became better known, though he himself preferred not to talk about it. When he was a Headmaster of a boys' secondary school in the 1950s, his pupils and their teachers knew nothing of his war record. Then, one evening, Francis was the subject of the well-known television programme, 'This Is Your Life'. Francis was tricked into coming to the studio where friends and colleagues, including some of his old comrades from the Maquis, were waiting to celebrate his wartime achievements. When Francis walked into the school hall to take morning assembly the next day, all the boys went wild, cheering their new and rather embarrassed hero.

Then there was another regular visitor, a Spitfire pilot who had survived the Battle of Britain. To a small boy at the end of the war, meeting a Spitfire pilot was as exciting as meeting David Beckham or Thierry Henry would be to a football fanatic today. Every time Michael's hero came to the house he was told he must not stare, because the pilot's face had been terribly burned and scarred in action. He had undergone extensive operations by plastic surgeons. However hard he tried, of course, six-year-old Michael could not take his eyes off that damaged face.

Michael has written several books about war. *War Horse*, *Farm Boy*, *The Butterfly Lion* and *Private Peaceful* all include the dramatic and sometimes terrible experiences of people, and animals, in the First World War. *Toro! Toro!* is set during the Spanish Civil War of 1936–39. *Billy the Kid* takes its reader through the North African desert, Italy and on to the horrors of the concentration camps in Germany in the Second World War. *Waiting for Anya* takes place in a German-occupied village in the French Pyrenees in the same war; and *The Amazing Story of Adolphus Tips* is told against the background of the tragic rehearsals in South Devon for the D-Day Landings of 1944. Looking back, Michael is sure his awareness of the parts his two uncles – and his Spitfire pilot hero – played in the war was an important element in firing his interest in the impact of war and its after-effects.

His uncles were influential in another way. Even when he was very young, Michael felt somehow that the sacrifice made by his Uncle Peter, and the mysterious bravery of his Uncle Francis, set high standards that he was supposed to live up to. Like

A school photo of Michael, 1948.

the Spitfire pilot, they had clearly had a strong sense of duty. Even now, despite all the stories he has written, all the prizes he has won and all his successful work for the charity, Farms for City Children, Michael still feels a strong pressure to succeed in whatever he does – and an anxiety that he might fail. Sometimes, that pressure can be helpful; at other times, it is a burden.

But it wasn't only his uncles who made him feel that kind of pressure as he grew older. A new and more powerful influence was about to enter Michael's life.

A Father, a Convict, a Polar Bear – and Another Father

Almost every home in Britain was affected in some way by the Second World War. Children who were evacuated often felt very homesick in their temporary families, miles away from those they loved. Children who stayed at home in the cities got used to the sight of enemy bombers in the night sky as they raced to the air-raid shelters, hurrying to put on their gas masks, which were often made with rubbery Mickey Mouse faces. Some lost a parent, a brother or a sister. Others, like Michael, grew up without knowing their fathers, away on active service overseas. Families who were bombed out of their homes had to live with relatives or in temporary accommodation for a while. Often it was several years after the war before the gaps in the streets of cities and suburbs were filled by new buildings.

The bomb-sites became exciting playgrounds for some children, and Michael was one of them. He went to a primary school close to his home in Philbeach

Gardens. Just next to the school was St Matthias' Chapel where Greek Orthodox priests lived with their severe black robes and long beards. Michael thought them mysterious and terrifying.

On the whole, though, he liked his new life in London. You weren't really allowed on a bomb-site – you never knew when a bit of a ruined building might collapse or there might even be an unexploded bomb among the debris. Michael and his friends made dens among the rubble and brambles, and the waste ground was good for playing hiding and chasing games and for fighting the war all over again.

London was full of daily excitements. Homes and factories used much more coal in those days, and sometimes you had to walk to school through a yellowy mist of fog and smoke ('smog', it was called) that used to hang eerily about the streets. It was so dense that all the traffic stopped and Michael could hardly see his hand in front of his face. Cars were not particularly common then and, anyway, petrol was still rationed. Even in the heart of London, the morning milk arrived at Philbeach Gardens on a cart pulled by Trumpeter, the first horse Michael ever knew personally.

Even though the war was over, food was still scarce. Chocolate and bananas were things you read about in stories or saw in comics – if you could find a comic to buy. All that the newsagents seemed to have were bags and bags of cough-sweets. Everyone had a ration book, and Michael remembers how important he felt when he was put in charge of the family's books on expeditions to the grocer's or the butcher's. He would present them to the shopkeeper, who would neatly mark the books with a crayoned cross. In return, Michael was given the small portions of meat or the slice or two of cheese which his family was allowed.

Michael and Peter in Philbeach Gardens, 1949.

Michael's move to Philbeach Gardens coincided with a huge upheaval in his family life, which turned out to have a powerful influence upon him. The war meant that husbands and wives were often apart for years on end, and when they were reunited they sometimes found things had changed between them. While Michael's father, Tony Bridge, was away overseas, Michael's mother had fallen in love with someone else.

Michael believes that when he was finally released from the Army, Tony Bridge saw little point in blaming his wife for what had happened. He still loved her and hoped to persuade her to start their life together again. They went off on a cycling holiday to Norfolk to see if they could sort things out. It was no good. Michael's father, a gentle and caring man, decided it was best for his two sons, who hardly knew him – and he hardly knew them – if he simply moved away. Then his wife, Peter and Michael could build a new family with the man who was to become the boys' stepfather, Jack Morpurgo. All he asked was that the boys should retain his surname; and Bridge is what the B in M.A.B. Morpurgo stands for.

So, reluctantly, Michael's father left. Divorce was seen as shameful in those days, and everyone involved agreed it would be best to avoid any kind of public scandal. But like so many of the stories that Michael spins, there were several unexpected twists to this one.

Before the war, Tony Bridge had been a student at the Royal Academy of Dramatic Arts, one of the best training schools for actors in the world. He was talented, and had spent a season before the war acting at the Royal Shakespeare Theatre in Stratford-upon-Avon. In 1948, he decided to leave England to work on an exciting project with a pioneering director, Tyrone Guthrie, establishing a new Shakespearian theatre at Stratford, Ontario in Canada.

So Tony Bridge seemed to have disappeared from his sons' lives before they ever knew him. But one Christmas, several years later and not long after the Morpurgos had bought their first television set, the family settled down to enjoy one of the special programmes broadcast over the holiday season. Watching television at that time was more of a family event than it is now. There was only one channel, and you had to draw the curtains to see the black-and-white pictures clearly. Everyone viewed together as a family – no remote control to play with, no commercial breaks and people tended not to drift in and out of the room. However, Jack Morpurgo did not think much of the quality of television programmes; he allowed the family just one per day.

The choice for that evening was a Canadian version of Charles Dickens' novel, *Great Expectations*. Right at the start, the young hero Pip is all alone one Christmas Eve in a churchyard where he's gone to visit the graves of his mother, father and five little brothers. Suddenly, with a blood-curdling yell, out from behind a tombstone leaps an absolutely terrifying figure: 'Hold your noise – Keep still, you little devil, or I'll cut your throat.' It's an escaped convict, 'soaked in water, and smothered in mud, and lamed by stones, and cut by flints and stung by nettles and torn by briars; who lunged and shivered and glared and growled; and whose teeth chattered in his head,' writes Dickens in the novel. No doubt Michael was just about as startled as poor Pip, when his mother suddenly grabbed his arm and shouted out, 'Oh, my God, that's your father, Michael!'

And so it was. There was no way of knowing what Tony Bridge, beneath the make-up, looked like. Thus Michael's first impression of his father was of a filthy, grotesque convict on the run, brandishing a knife.

Years later, when he was acting in London, Tony Bridge decided the time had come to meet his sons. At last, Michael had something more to work with than an image of a murderous criminal. Since that meeting, Michael, Clare and their three children have kept in regular contact with Tony Bridge, who continued his successful acting career in Canada well into his 80s.

Long after they had got to know one another, Michael came across an old copy of a magazine called

Theatre World. It fell open at a photograph of his father in a scene from a play for children – or, at least, the caption *said* it was his father; this time Tony Bridge was wearing a polar bear costume and mask. Michael was an experienced writer by then, with a keen eye for a good story when he saw one. So he brought his older brother Peter – who had always wanted to be an actor like his father – into the plot, and told a story about a small stage-struck boy whose first glimpses of his actor father are as an escaped convict and as a polar bear. The story, 'My Father is a Polar Bear', is included in Michael's collection of short stories, *From Hereabout Hill*.

*   *   *

Jack Morpurgo, Michael's stepfather, was not an easy person for a small boy to get on with. He had grown up in a Jewish family with little money to spare in the East End of London. His mother had died when he was still a child, and the rest of his family concentrated all their hopes on young Jack. He was very bright and won a scholarship to Christ's Hospital School, near Horsham in Sussex, which offered a boarding school education to boys whose parents could not afford the fees normally charged by private schools. Here, Jack Morpurgo worked fiercely, and successfully, to reach the high standards the school

Michael on a family holiday in France, 1950.

demanded in everything the boys attempted in the classroom, on the sports field and in the daily social life of the school.

After university in Canada and the United States, Jack had fought in the Second World War, seeing front line action in the North African desert and in Italy as the Allies slowly pushed northwards towards Germany. He had done well, and left the Army at the end of the war with the rank of Major. Jack's years at Christ's Hospital and in the Army were the most intense and influential of his life, shaping everything else he did. And everything he wanted his new step-sons to do too. He was a strong believer in firm discipline and in setting the highest targets for them in whatever challenges they faced.

After the war, Jack Morpurgo worked as a History Editor for Penguin, the famous book publisher, at an exciting time when the firm was making paperback books available to a wider public at inexpensive prices. It was Penguin who, in 1941, produced the first series of low-priced paperbacks for children under the imprint of Puffin Books.

Later, Jack Morpurgo was Director of the National Book League and after that he became Professor of American Literature at Leeds University. He broadcast regularly on BBC Radio, where he was a competitor in *Round Britain Quiz*, a programme which is still broadcast today. Understanding the questions is difficult enough, never mind working out the answers.

Jack Morpurgo was used to fighting for everything he achieved. He seemed to succeed in whatever he did, though nothing ever satisfied him. When he was at home, Jack seemed always to be in his study writing another book. When two more children, Mark and Kay, came along to join his stepsons, he took his responsibilities as father and stepfather seriously. But what he couldn't do was spend time comfortably with his children – to have fun with them, to talk with them or to let them be themselves, especially when they chose to behave differently from the ways he had known as a boy. Because he trusted strongly in what had worked for him, it seemed logical to him that all his children should follow closely in his footsteps.

As he grew up, Michael wanted desperately to please his stepfather. Firstly, because he respected Jack Morpurgo and what he had achieved. Secondly, because pleasing his stepfather was a way of pleasing his mother, which he was also very keen to do. And thirdly, because this was the way to keep the peace at home. Michael always felt that however hard he tried to please his stepfather, he could never manage to do enough. Looking back, Michael does not blame his stepfather for making such heavy demands on his children. Apart from anything else, being a parent himself has taught Michael just how difficult it is to get things right. He knows that Jack Morpurgo genuinely believed he was making the best choices for his children. It was just that he set such high standards and he was so difficult to approach that they were frightened of him, and felt miserable when they failed to come up to the mark.

Jack's standards applied even to the books Michael was expected to read. Not many young children enjoy books usually read by adults, but Jack Morpurgo had been one of them. Now he believed his stepsons should read what he had enjoyed as a boy. Jack Morpurgo thought that books by 19th-century writers such as Anthony Trollope or Charles Dickens would be just the thing for young Michael. In fact, most of the authors his stepfather approved of had been dead for at least 100 years, which meant that the English they wrote was not the English Michael spoke and understood.

From time to time, Jack would question Michael about what he was supposed to have read. Even to please his stepfather, Michael couldn't manage to get through the hundreds of pages of small print in the books he was expected to read. So, he cheated. By wonderful luck, he came across a series of comics published at that time called *Classics Illustrated*. They told the stories of those long, long books in exciting, colourful pictures with speech bubbles, rather like *Beano* and *Dandy*. With the help of *Classics Illustrated*, Michael just about scraped through his stepfather's cross-examinations. Meanwhile, he smuggled into the house odd copies of other comics and Enid Blyton's Famous Five or Secret Seven series. Under the bed-clothes or wherever his stepfather would not find him, he could escape to the wild west of Desperate Dan, to Kirrin Island or Smuggler's Top.

And then, one day, a miracle! He found a book which he loved and which Jack Morpurgo thoroughly approved of: Robert Louis Stevenson's *Treasure Island*. Adventure on the high seas, buried treasure, pirates, Long John Silver with his 200-year-old parrot, Cap'n Flint, screaming, 'Pieces of eight! Pieces of eight!' It was all terrific! Most chilling of all was the terrifying Blind Pew tap-tap-tapping his way with his stick to the Admiral Benbow Inn to deliver the dreaded black spot to the rum-soaked Billy Bones. No sooner is the black spot in Billy's palm than the old sea-dog 'reeled, put his hand to his throat, stood swaying for a moment, and then, with a peculiar sound, fell from his whole height face foremost to the floor … The captain had been struck dead by thundering apoplexy.' Michael loved it all; he read the book again and again. And then, again. Even better, he could please his stepfather knowing he wasn't having to cheat. One Robert Louis Stevenson led to another. Michael went on to *Kidnapped* to discover the swash-buckling Highlander, Alan Breck Stewart and a tale of treachery, shipwreck, murder, flashing swordplay and a desperate flight across the heather. He loved that one too.

Michael had met Robert Louis Stevenson when he was much younger, for his mother and grandmother used to read poems from Stevenson's *A Child's Garden of Verses* to him. To this day, Robert Louis Stevenson is one of his writer-heroes.

Eleven or twelve years passed before Michael loved another story with the excitement he had found in *Treasure Island* and *Kidnapped*.

Sink or Swim

Since Christ's Hospital School had been very important in the making of Jack Morpurgo, he decided that Peter and Michael in their turn should be sent away to prep schools. In the boarding school system, pupils attend a preparatory school until they are thirteen; then they move on to a public school, usually until they are eighteen.

People have very different views about boarding schools, including those who attend them or used to attend them. For some, their school days are the happiest days of their lives; for others, the worst. Those who have not been pupils at boarding schools may think they involve endless games of Quidditch, bossy girls called Hermione and ghosts whose heads haven't quite parted from their shoulders. For Michael, going off to his prep school each term was not remotely like catching the Hogwarts Express from Platform Nine and three-quarters. When he first went, he was only seven years old. He was miserably homesick. Just how much he hated school is very clear when you read *The War of Jenkins' Ear*, which begins with Toby Jenkins locking himself in the toilet to sob his heart out as the train leaves Victoria Station *en route* for a new term away at boarding school.

'My One and Only Great Escape', a story in a collection by ten different writers called *Ten of the Best*, is based very closely on Michael's own experiences. By the time he was sent to prep school, the Morpurgo family had moved yet again, this time to Bradwell-on-Sea in Essex. Michael loved his summers there, exploring the seashore and the marshes or playing in the family's large house with his brother. Then, ten days before he had to go back to school, his mother would begin the slow process of packing his school trunk. Michael would feel physically sick, dreading the terrible day when the journey to Sussex via London began. The worst moment was when he saw the vast sea of school caps from so many different prep schools at the station. Everyone else seemed glad to be going back – they were all laughing and shouting and greeting each other. 'Going up the escalator into the bustling smoky concourse of Victoria Station was as I imagined it might be going up the steps on to the scaffold to face my executioner', writes Michael in 'My One and Only Great Escape'. Once on the train, Michael was forced to lock himself in the toilet to hide his tears from his jeering school-fellows, just like Toby Jenkins.

Like the narrator in *The Butterfly Lion*, Michael once ran away from school, only to meet an elderly lady who fed him tea and cakes and gently persuaded him to go back. You have to survive somehow and like most children who have been miserable at any kind of school at some time or another, Michael found a way of swimming rather than sinking. He never learned to enjoy his prep school days, but there were good bits outside the classroom which helped him get by. At prep school, and later at public school, you have to play team sports most afternoons, which is fine if you like games and are good at them, but a nightmare if you don't and are not. Luckily for Michael, he enjoyed sports and ended up as vice-captain of the rugby team and captain of cricket at his prep school. He also liked singing and was good at that too, and there was plenty of singing at both his prep school and his public school.

In class, he tried to be as invisible as possible. The masters ruled by fear, and Michael was afraid of looking stupid in front of the other boys. Tests were frequent and important, and Michael was usually down near the bottom of the class. As far as stories or poems went, he doesn't remember enjoying anything at all which was read in class. In fact, one of the very worst times for him was when the teacher made the boys read aloud around the class, up and down the rows of desks, a paragraph at a time. His turn came relentlessly closer and closer and then – the focus was on him. Michael hated it so much that he developed a severe stutter when he had to read. He couldn't get his 'r's out properly and his 't's seemed to trip over his tongue. As the Children's Laureate, he has been particularly concerned for children who are just the way he was 50 years ago. How are you supposed to *enjoy* a book if you're scared stiff of looking like an idiot when you read aloud or can't answer questions which come at you like machine-gun bullets?

But since he was good at sports and singing and equally good at doing what he was told and keeping out of trouble, the teachers decided that young Morpurgo was a Good Chap. Not very bright maybe, but certainly a Good All-Rounder. Decent sort of fellow.

At thirteen, he moved on to The King's School, Canterbury, a famous public school. Although schools like King's or Eton, which Prince William and Prince Harry attended, are called 'public' schools, they are in fact 'private'. You can go there only if you pass an entrance exam and, unless you win a scholarship, your parents must pay substantial fees. Michael's brother, Peter, was sent off to Derbyshire to board at Abbotsholme School. He had found even more difficulty than Michael in pleasing his stepfather, since he was not so good at games and being a Good All-Rounder. He had wanted to be an actor since he was very young, however, and he found consolation at

Abbotsholme in taking part in school plays and singing in Gilbert and Sullivan comic operas. All the family would help in rehearsing his lines during school holidays. Michael does not feel proud about the way he sometimes treated his brother during their boyhood. 'I was always the boisterous, showy-off one', he says. 'Peter was much quieter and nicer, but I tended to get the attention.' Fortunately, as they grew older, the brothers became, and remain, good friends.

At King's, Michael continued to employ his survival tactics. He excelled at sports, was enthusiastic about music and drew as little attention to himself in lessons as he could. Discipline was strict and the school 'uniform' of stiff-winged collar, black jacket and pinstripe trousers reflected the formal behaviour which was expected of the boys. In time, Michael found that he was doing better than just surviving and he values much of what King's gave him.

The school is housed in lovely medieval buildings and the boys sang frequently in the nearby Canterbury Cathedral. It is impossible to be unaffected by the beauty of such a setting when it is a part of your daily life. Much of Michael's love of music, and the arts in general, was developed during his time at King's. He particularly admired the Headmaster, Fred Shirley, and two or three of the teaching staff who saw more promise in Michael, perhaps, than he saw in himself. He recalls an inspiring music teacher, an English teacher who never talked down to him, and a German teacher who sat with his class on the lawns outside the old buildings, playing them records of Mozart's *Magic Flute* before they studied the German text. These were the people who saved him from drowning, along with the occasional experience outside school.

Once, in the school holidays, for example, when he was twelve or thirteen, Michael found himself wandering through the theatre district in London's West End. He'd had a row about his school report and stomped out of the house to be on his own. As he passed the Phoenix Theatre, he saw that a well-known actor, Paul Schofield, was playing in Shakespeare's *Hamlet*. Michael had seen the Laurence Olivier film of the play, but he had never seen a stage performance. He had just about enough money for a cheap seat, so in he went. He has never forgotten that impulsive decision – listening to the rhythms of Paul Schofield's voice as Prince Hamlet was magical. It wasn't so much the meaning of what he said, but the music in the way he said it. And somehow that connected with his memories of his mother reading 'The Elephant's Child' and even his own excited discovery of *Treasure Island*.

At boarding school, unless you're very unlucky, you make plenty of good friends and spend almost all day, every day, with them. If you like playing games, you play nearly every day and you often have good coaching too. There is time to follow your interests in different clubs and societies. On the other hand, you don't see your family for about eight months of the year, except when they come to visit you a couple of weekends each term. Most of the pupils come from similar backgrounds, so your range of friends is limited. And in Michael's day, most public schools were either all boys or all girls. This meant that he saw little of one half of the human race for term after term, and he now thinks that this led – for a while at least – to a rather lopsided view of life. To correct this imbalance at King's, occasional dances were organised with Benenden School, an equally famous girls' public school not far away – Princess Anne was educated there. Michael thought of these encounters rather as if they were sports fixtures, that King's were dancing *against* Benenden. The boys lined up on one side of the dining hall and the girls faced them on the other, with the masters and mistresses circling around them like watchful referees to see that no fouls were committed, except when the masters and mistresses were circling round each other!

Michael's stepfather was pleased with Michael's progress. The teaching staff thought well of him and he was generally playing the game by the rules.

Indeed, they thought Michael was such a Good Chap that he was made Captain of School – a major honour, bringing with it responsibilities for running the

Michael with HRH Queen Elizabeth, The Queen Mother, at King's School, Canterbury, 1962.

prefect system, which is very important in the daily organisation of public schools.

Through his sport and his music, and through being Captain of School and his friendships, he developed a strong sense of confidence. He learned that if you want to do something, you should go ahead and try it – and you'll probably achieve it. This is not about being conceited. Michael simply knew he could trust his own ability. 'I felt', he says, 'that I could do *anything*.' Outside the classroom, at least.

What Jack Morpurgo never saw, though, was that Michael was not at all *excited* by what he was being taught in the classroom. He didn't really expect to be – excitement was not what schoolwork was about. This would seem odd to anyone meeting Michael now, for one thing you cannot miss about him is that he is frequently excited by life, that he lives it with an enthusiasm he likes to share with those he meets and those who read his books.

Far from being excited, Michael was often anxious in lessons, just as he had been at prep school. Once again, the main thing was to be noticed as little as possible, but that was not easy. Every two weeks, the boys in each class were ranked in order according to their marks in written work. There were also regular reports from tutors. Michael would lie awake in his dormitory worrying whether he had done enough to escape attention. He does not remember reading a single book which gave him a sense of pleasure, either inside the classroom or out. Nevertheless, he eventually took English at A-level, which required him to read the works of some of the great novelists, poets and playwrights. Here, he was asked to analyse books so closely that there was little chance that he could enjoy them at the same time. For Michael, Shakespeare was dead on the page, not alive on the stage; this kind of study had nothing to do with the magic of Paul Schofield playing Hamlet. Writing was always very difficult. He tried to do what he thought his teachers asked him to do, but he never wrote something which he actually *wanted* to write. He was particularly baffled when English teachers used to say to him, 'Use your imagination, Morpurgo!' That seemed an impossibly mysterious instruction to him and now, when he visits schools, he finds it depressing that some of the things children are asked to do in their writing lessons seem to him just as impossible.

King's was always near the top of the league table, printed each year in the newspapers, recording how many pupils from schools around the country had been accepted at Oxford and Cambridge universities. King's boys often went on after university to become lawyers, doctors, businessmen or clergymen. Michael was not considered intellectually bright enough to try for Oxford or Cambridge – or for any other university

Michael, far left, about to meet Nehru, the first Prime Minister of independent India, as a young cadet, 1961.

for that matter. The route ahead seemed clear to Michael's parents and his teachers. He had done well in the Army Cadet Force at school, showing he was good at leading and organising other boys. He had been promoted to the rank of Company Sergeant Major, the highest a boy could reach. He was, he says, 'good at marching up and down and telling other people what to do'. Jack Morpurgo and Michael's two uncles had served with distinction in the war. 'So,' says Michael, 'because they thought I was a Bear of Very Little Brain, they thought, fine, Michael will do very well in the Army!'

At sixteen, Michael won a scholarship offered by the Army, who then contributed to his school fees for his last two years at King's. Then he was all set to enter the Royal Military Academy, Sandhurst, to train as an Army officer.

The Army, a Rubbish Heap and a Surprising Change of Plan

Nineteen years of age, a Sandhurst cadet and a promising career in the Army in front of him. Plenty of sport, plenty of new friends, plenty of marching up and down and, once he had passed his training course, plenty of telling other people what to do. What more could Michael want?

But fortunately for all of us who enjoy his stories, and even more fortunately for Michael, things didn't work out. They didn't work out largely because of a conversation the summer before Michael started at Sandhurst, when he was standing on top of a rubbish heap late one evening on the Greek island of Corfu.

Michael was on holiday on the island with his family. When Jack Morpurgo had worked at Penguin Books, he had become friendly with the firm's founder, Sir Allen Lane. By coincidence, two of Allen Lane's four daughters were also holidaying on Corfu, so Jack Morpurgo took Michael with him to pay a social call on the girls. Michael isn't quite sure now exactly *why* he was standing on the rubbish heap in the half-dark, but he does know that the heap was outside the hotel where Allen Lane's daughters were staying. A rubbish heap may seem an odd place to meet your wife-to-be, but that's where Michael was standing when he and Clare had their first conversation. For her part, Clare was leaning out of the hotel window.

Michael made an immediate impression on Clare. So much so that she even came down to join Michael and his stepfather on the rubbish heap and, after the visitors had gone, she went back into the hotel and told her sister, 'He's just right for you!' Later that holiday, the Morpurgos and the Lanes met again and Clare and Michael got to know each other a little better.

Back home in England, Michael was soon off to start his promising Army career. Sandhurst was good for him, he thinks. You had to train hard, you had to get very fit and the Army removed any sense of self-importance the former Captain of King's School, Canterbury might have had. When a Sergeant Major from the Coldstream Guards screamed, 'Mr Morpurgo, sir! If you are late on parade again I shall castrate you with the rough end of a ragman's trumpet!' Michael got the general idea, even if he wasn't exactly sure what the Sergeant Major meant. He could see that, in the Sergeant Major's opinion, he was not the centre of the universe. 'Mucking in' with others going through the tough training course led to strong friendships, some of which have lasted to the present day.

The trouble was that however busy he was, Michael could not stop thinking about Clare. She had been studying in Paris for a year, but now she was back in London taking her A-levels. They wrote letters, they telephoned (no text messages or e-mails in those days) and they met whenever they could. Talking and falling in love with Clare made Michael think. Think for himself. Just what was he doing at Sandhurst? Everything he was being trained to do led, in the end, to killing people. Was that how he wanted to spend his life? In fact, had he ever seriously thought about what *he* wanted to do, or had others decided for him? It was his life, after all.

His questioning was suddenly cut short. There was a decision which could not be delayed. Clare was going to have their baby and she and Michael wanted to get married. Clare's family was very upset and Jack Morpurgo would not even speak to Michael – all his hopes for his stepson were in ruins. But Michael's mother came to the rescue; 'She loved Clare to bits, right from the start', says Michael. So Mother hatched a plot with her son. Hatching plots has never been a problem for Michael and it clearly wasn't too difficult for his mother, either.

Michael and Clare in 1962.

Mrs Morpurgo sent a telegram to Officer Cadet Morpurgo at Sandhurst: 'MOTHER DANGER-OUSLY ILL. COME IMMEDIATELY.' Obviously, a visit home to the bedside of a desperately sick mother was essential. Could Officer Cadet Morpurgo be granted some compassionate leave? The trick worked.

Michael was given his leave by his Company Commander. He came home and the couple were married at Kensington Registry Office. They managed a one-night honeymoon by the River Thames at Marlow and Michael even found time to fail his driving test as well. On his return to Sandhurst, he had to admit to his new status as a married man. The rules were that a cadet at Sandhurst was not allowed to be married. Those were the rules and, in the Army, you can't change the rules. Within 24 hours, 9 months after he had arrived, Michael was packing his bags. No more marching up and down and no more telling other people what to do. Although he did not know it then, his spell at Sandhurst had not been wasted time. It left him with an understanding of how the Army works and how soldiers think and behave as a result of their training. Such insights proved useful to him when he was writing his stories set during times of war.

Although the tension between Michael and his stepfather eased in time, Michael knew he had bitterly disappointed him. Michael and Clare very much regretted that, but it could not be helped. Michael had begun to realise that although he admired Jack's great drive to succeed in whatever he attempted, it made him very difficult to live with. Michael and Clare knew they had to lead their own lives, to find their own way. And what's more, they would soon have a baby to care for.

A Green Giant, Caning and a Grey Heron

If this were a fairy tale, the twenty-year-old Michael would suddenly realise that he had always wanted to be a children's writer. He would dash off his first prize-winning bestseller. Hollywood directors would beg him to allow them to film his story and, in due course, the movie would collect a mantelpiece full of Oscars. The truth is that Michael was just married, his Army career had vanished, he was struggling to win the confidence of Clare's family and slowly sorting things out with Jack Morpurgo. Michael had no thoughts of writing a book. In fact, even *reading* a book was not particularly important to him at that time.

How could he earn a living? Well, much of his life had been spent in boarding schools, and you could teach in a prep school even if you had no qualifications. He and Clare found jobs at Great Ballard Preparatory School in Sussex. Clare taught art, while Michael says he taught 'this, that and the other'. Most teachers would rather forget their first few months in the classroom, but Michael can't quite do that. Every time he visits his local pub, the Duke of York in Iddesleigh (the pub and the village come into several of his stories), he meets the landlord, Jamie Stuart. Forty years ago, young Jamie sat behind his desk in Michael's class at Great Ballard Prep School. He still has a school report written by Michael. These days, pupil and teacher are the best of friends.

It wasn't long before Michael realised that he would need qualifications if he wanted to make a career in teaching. He applied for a place at King's College, London University, where he was accepted to study French, English and Philosophy. Clare and Michael rented a flat in London (yet another new home) and Michael found himself catching the tube to college every day along with all the office workers. If you have a wife and baby son, it's difficult to enjoy the social life of a student outside the classroom. So he attended his lectures and then caught the train home again. He is very modest about his academic achievements at the university. 'I just about hung in there', he says. Studying was no easier for him than it had been during his schooldays.

However, he took two valuable experiences away from university with him. First, he improved his ability to speak and read French. Michael's books have been translated into 26 languages, but he is especially

Proud parents Michael and Clare, with Canon Fred Shirley
at baby Sebastian's Christening, 1964.

popular in France. Even in small towns, the news-
agent's or the bookshop usually has at least a couple
of his books for sale, and sometimes many more. Two
of his books, *Arthur, High King of Britain* and *Farm Boy*
(published as *Secrets de Grandpère*) are on the French
equivalent of the National Curriculum. He makes
four or five trips a year to France to talk, in French,
about his books to children, teachers and librarians.

Another university experience, which he has never
forgotten, occurred in one of his English classes. The
students were looking at a long poem, written in the

fourteenth century, telling the adventures of one of the knights of King Arthur's round table. It is called *Sir Gawain and the Green Knight*.

The story begins in the Christmas season, when Arthur's court at Camelot enjoys fifteen days of feasting and storytelling. Each evening, before the company is allowed to sit down to enjoy a marvellous feast, it is the tradition that the king must hear a tale of romance or high adventure. So on New Year's Day, Arthur asks who is willing to tell a story that evening. Before anyone can reply, the doors of the hall burst open and a huge man comes in, towering over the assembled lords and their ladies. He hasn't bothered to dismount from his horse, even in the presence of the king. As if that were not a big enough shock, this giant of a man is green from head to toe. Not just his clothes, but his skin, his hair, his beard, his armour – everything is bright green. Fierce insults and challenges follow, a head gets chopped off and used as a football (though not in an actual game), an evil sorceress spins a cunning plot and Sir Gawain has to undertake an arduous journey with some very surprising adventures at the end of it.

The old tale caught Michael's imagination in the way no story had really captivated him since *Treasure Island* when he was nine years old. Without fully realising what was happening, Michael began at last to read in the way he still reads today. He reads quickly – he is an explorer, discovering new ideas, living through new experiences, eager to find out what happens when a character chooses this road, or maybe that one – and wondering what *he* would have done in their shoes. If readers don't read with enjoyment and with excitement, then Michael thinks they are missing out on one of life's most vital experiences. It's because he feels *he* missed out for far too long that he cares so much about his work as Children's Laureate. It matters. He is convinced that, from the aboriginal peoples in Australia to the crowds on the streets of Beijing, from the Inuit in the Arctic to the office workers of London and New York, everyone has a need for stories. Good stories are at the centre of how people make sense of who they are and how they live with other people and the world around them. If people don't have stories, Michael believes, they are living only half a life.

University over, Michael went back to teaching in another prep school – Milner Court, just outside Canterbury. By now, he was constantly reading novels, poems and plays written for young people. He re-read some of the stories he hadn't much enjoyed when he was growing up; it was like reading different books altogether – this time around he thoroughly enjoyed them. What's more, he desperately wanted his pupils to enjoy reading as much as he was.

As he read, he came across a book about children and writing called *Poetry in the Making*. Its author was Ted Hughes, a famous poet who also wrote stories for children – his best known book is *The Iron Man*. *Poetry in the Making* was based on a series of BBC Radio talks Ted Hughes gave for children and teachers, which Michael and his class used to listen to. His own pupils had begun to produce some very exciting writing. Now, what Ted Hughes said in his book made sense of what Michael was finding out, following his own intuition, in the classroom. Michael sent some of the poems his boys had written to the BBC and, before long, he was regularly taking four or five boys up to London to read their poems for the radio broadcasts.

Despite his excitement about his teaching, Michael found working in the prep school posed some serious problems for him. He disliked many of the rules and regulations. Above all, he did not like the way discipline was maintained by fear and the threat of the cane. It brought back too many memories of his own prep school days when any boy caught out of bed after 'lights out' would be thrashed. Michael can still hear the agonised shrieks of the victims to this day. In his story, *The War of Jenkins' Ear*, the new boy, Christopher, is beaten ferociously by Mr Stagg, the Headmaster – Mr Stagg is based on the Head at Milner Court. One day, Michael decided that the Head's cruelty had gone too far. He reported his brutal behaviour to the governors. The governors preferred to believe the Head rather than the young teacher and sacked Michael. Fortunately, he was a member of a teachers' union which came to his defence and forced the governors to reverse their decision. Whereupon, honour satisfied and with no blot on his record, Michael resigned his position and left the school. Apart from his problems over the violence of the discipline, he had begun to feel uncomfortable with the fact that Milner Court was a fee-paying school, and that meant only boys from wealthy families could attend.

Michael now qualified as a teacher by taking a correspondence course. Then, it was time for him to take a post in a state primary school, where he would teach girls as well as boys. This time, the children came from many different backgrounds. The new experience proved to be very important in developing the way Michael and Clare thought about education and, as it turned out, in shaping their whole future together.

Outside school, Michael saw his own growing family – Sebastian and Horatio by now had been joined by Rosalind – loving the times when their mother and father read stories to them. Sometimes Michael would make up stories to tell them, and they loved that too. Once they started reading on their own, they couldn't wait to talk with their parents about what they read. They were not just having fun together – there was something very powerful about these reading times, something which really mattered. Stories were at the centre of their family life.

Michael with Sebastian, 1966.

Clare holding Horatio, 1968.

Clare admiring Ros at her christening, 1969.

Now, in his new school, Wickhambreaux, again near Canterbury, Michael was lucky enough to have a Headmaster who also knew about the power of stories. 'I want you to let the children have a quiet time at the end of every day,' he told his staff, 'when you simply read to them. Half an hour a day, if you like.' Michael did just that and found that the children always looked forward to that time. He knew that he and his class were listening, talking and learning together – and thoroughly enjoying themselves while they were about it. So, just as stories were at the centre of his family life, they were now also at the centre of the life of his class in school.

Then, one afternoon, something happened that changed the direction of Michael's teaching and, when he looks back on it, the direction of his life. This is how he describes a lesson at the end of one particular day when his Year Six class had settled down for Michael to read to them, as the Headmaster recommended:

I was sitting in my mobile classroom, which hadn't moved anywhere for about 25 years, and I was reading this story. Before too long, I realised they weren't enjoying it. The one golden rule I had already learned was – Never Bore Them. But they were shuffling about, picking their noses and looking out of the window. It wasn't working. So I tried to put more into the way I was reading it – you know, more variety in my voice, a bit more emphasis, and so on. No good. So, I went home and told Clare about it that night. 'Look,' I said, 'I've got fourteen more chapters of this wretched book to read – it's just not working!'

Not for the last time, Clare came to his rescue. She pointed out that he was pretty good at *telling* his own stories before bedtime to Sebastian, Horatio and Rosalind, so why didn't he go into school the next day and try telling his class a story he'd made up himself – with no book between him and them?

Michael decided he'd give it a try. But that night, he kept waking up, turning over in his mind the story he was still trying to make up and worrying that the Year Sixes might eat him alive if it didn't work. When 3 o'clock came around the next day, he announced that he was not going to read the book to them any more. Of course, they immediately told him how much they'd been enjoying it, as any Year Six class would. 'Too bad,' said Michael, 'I've made up this story for you now, and you're getting it whether you like it or not.'

So he began his story. Almost at once, their faces changed. They even seemed to be sitting differently! They were all focused on the story and the storyteller. Michael was excited by what was happening. He could almost touch the atmosphere, the concentration was so powerful. It wasn't so much that it was a wonderful story – it wasn't bad, but Michael knew it needed a lot more work and time. The great thing was that his class knew that their teacher was committed to the story, they could see he was excited about it – the power lay in the way the tale was told as well as the tale itself. This kind of storytelling was like live theatre.

He continued the story from one day to the next, like a serial on television or radio. One of Michael's friends, another teacher in the school, had written some textbooks for Macmillan, the publisher. When he heard about what was happening in Michael's classroom, he urged him to send his story to Macmillan's education department. Michael worked hard to retell his story in written form, while trying to preserve the voice of the live storyteller. He sent it off to Aidan Chambers, an editor at Macmillan. Aidan wrote Michael a letter which mattered a great deal – it was very encouraging, especially as Aidan was a fine writer and a teacher himself. He told Michael how much he had enjoyed reading the story, and how pleased he would be to publish it. Over the next few years, Michael wrote several stories for Macmillan. His writing career had begun.

Now Michael wanted all his pupils not only to read with enthusiasm, he wanted them to write with the same excitement that he had discovered for himself. As a boy at school, he had tried very hard to write what he thought the teachers wanted him to write. That had always been difficult; the work didn't mean anything to him – it was just another exercise. Now he knew that was the wrong way to go about writing. He didn't want the children in his class simply to write correctly, to know how to use adverbs or connectives or semicolons. He wanted more than that. Of course he knew it was necessary for them to get their grammar right – to spell accurately and to punctuate well – but first he hoped they would write because they *wanted* to, because they had something to say that mattered to them. As *Poetry in the Making* advised, they should write about themselves, about what they saw around them in their daily lives, about their families and friends, about their thoughts and feelings. If you write about what matters to you, Michael still believes, then you will want to present your work as well as possible – and that means that before you finish a piece, you will want it to be well punctuated and correctly spelt.

One day, determined to put the ideas he had met in *Poetry in the Making* into practice, Michael took his class out to a nature reserve near the school. When they reached a lake, he told them to find a spot on their own and to settle down. 'Just listen and watch. Nobody talks, just keep listening and keep watching.' The children crouched down close to the reeds and listened to the silence. Except, of course, they soon found that there was no such thing as silence. Instead, there were all sorts of noises they were usually too busy to hear. Then, like an actor on cue, a grey heron came wheeling down on its huge wings, and began to fish, only about twenty metres from where the children were. They watched the great bird stalking through the shallows. Then it stopped and stood like a statue, waiting for its prey. The long beak came stabbing down a couple of times and the watching children could even see the bulge in its neck as the heron swallowed. Eventually, the bird lifted out of the water and took its heavy flight away over the lake.

After a while, Michael told the children to get up quietly and make their way back to the school. 'And,' he insisted, 'Nobody Talks to Anyone Else.' Back to school they went and, in silence, sat down to write. Michael also wrote about what he had seen and heard. Then they all read what they had written to each other. It was one of those lessons when all the children in the class and the teacher know that everyone is glad to be doing just what they are. No one wanted the bell to go.

Throughout that year, he says, he and his class were growing up together as writers.

He was excited by what was happening. Experiences like the one by the lake made Michael think about what children learned when they were *outside* as well as inside the classroom. After all, he had learned most when he was at school outside the classroom … the singing, the rugby and cricket, the cadet force, the friendships, the chats with teachers outside lessons. Was it somehow possible for him to teach children outside rather than inside the four walls of a classroom?

Michael reading to Ros and Horatio, 1973.

A Place to Belong

Clare's father, Sir Allen Lane, the founder of Penguin Books, had died in 1970, leaving a large sum of money at Clare's disposal. Clare believed that if you were fortunate enough to have money, especially if you hadn't earned it yourself, you had a responsibility to share your good fortune with others. She had been educated at a boarding school run by the Quakers, the religious group also known as The Society of Friends. Clare admired the work of Quakers in earlier centuries, such as Elizabeth Fry who worked tirelessly to improve conditions in prisons and to provide shelter for the homeless in the early 1800s. A basic belief of the Quakers was that you should share whatever you have – your time, talents, money and possessions.

Allen Lane's bequest provided the opportunity for Clare and Michael to put their ideas about education outside the classroom into practice; and to use the money in a way that, they knew, would have given

Clare's father satisfaction. Both Michael and Clare loved the countryside – and as they talked about their future, they wondered whether they could somehow share that love of the countryside with children. Clare had spent some of her childhood on a farm and she had also enjoyed many holidays staying at the Duke of York at Iddesleigh in north-west Devon. The lady who ran the pub, Peggy Rafferty, was Clare's 'unofficial godmother'. During her visits to Peggy, sometimes with her parents and sometimes on her own, Clare had grown to love the lanes, the streams, the farms and the animals around Iddesleigh. Many of the local people were now her friends.

Michael and Clare's plans began to take shape. How could other children know the pleasure and excitement Clare had known on those childhood holidays? Who would benefit most – maybe children who spent all their lives in cities, who had never had the chance to explore the countryside? They spent hours talking their ideas through with friends and other teachers. They went up to Leeds University, where Jack Morpurgo now taught American Literature, and met professors in the education department. The experts thought their ideas made good sense – they too knew that experiences outside the classroom are often vitally important in a child's education.

Michael and Clare were encouraged and excited. What they needed now was the right place – and the right place suddenly came on the market. Nethercott House, just outside Iddesleigh, with some 50 acres of farming land, was for sale. The money Clare had been left by her father was enough to buy the property, and Michael and Clare travelled down to Devon to talk with the Wards, the farming family who rented the Nethercott land for their animals and their crops. The Wards were enthusiastic about the idea of becoming involved in bringing children down for a week on a working farm.

The scheme they devised was that children from primary schools in the cities would come down to Nethercott for a week – about 30 children at a time. They would work on a real farm alongside real farmers and real animals. They would be involved in everything from mucking out the pigs to picking potatoes, from laying hedges to digging ditches. They might see the birth of a calf or a lamb. They would work in all weathers, properly clothed for the job, just like the local people who spent their lives living and working in the countryside. They might learn to press apples, or how to make cheese. They would see that carrots grow in fields rather than on supermarket shelves, that milk comes from cows' udders rather than plastic bottles with different coloured tops. They would also have time to explore the fields, the lanes and the streams, just as Clare had done. On a clear night, they would be able to gaze up at the stars, bright against the velvet black of the sky, undimmed by the light spilling from street lamps and houses. At least once during their week, when they were relaxing at the end of a day's work and play, Michael would either read to them or tell his stories around the fire. The children would write too – what happened to them during their days on the farm would surely give them plenty they wanted to write about.

Michael and Clare and the children moved to a new home close to Nethercott. They spent a year working with the local farmers, learning how to farm themselves. Then, in January 1976, the first group of children, from Chivenor Primary School in Birmingham, came down. The timetable Michael and Clare set themselves was exhausting. At the end of their week's stay, a group would leave on a Friday morning at 9 o'clock and at 2.30 pm the next group would arrive. Groups have been arriving, every Friday in term-time, ever since. The Ward family are still enthusiastic – when the scheme started, they had 200 acres available for the visitors' use along with Nethercott's 50. Now there are 500 acres. Two more Farms for City Children are in full operation: Lower Treginnis on the wild Pembrokeshire coast in the far west of Wales and Wick Court, a magical Elizabethan manor house in Gloucestershire.

The staff at Nethercott increased. Peggy Rafferty

and her husband, Sean, retired from the pub and came to live and work on the Nethercott estate. Over the years, the two families became increasingly close friends, often sharing meals and Christmases together. As they grew up, the Morpurgo children spent hours at the Raffertys' cottage, simply talking. Mrs Weeks, the cook from the Duke of York (and it was – and still is – one of the best places to eat in Devon) came to prepare meals for the children.

How Michael has managed to write so many books remains a mystery, even to those who know him well. He is full of energy and hates to be bored, and has therefore always enjoyed the crowded variety of his life. Most of all, he would hate to be bored by his own writing, and so is always looking out for a new story to tell. Nethercott and the children who come to stay there feed his stories. *Sam's Duck*, a picture book with illustrations by Keith Bowen, begins with a boy from the city who is dreading spending a week on his school's visit to Nethercott. Once he has arrived in Devon, Sam has no choice but to work, and work he does. He has no time to be homesick. In fact, he loves every minute; he even helps with the birth of a lamb. But, when the class goes off to the local market, he secretly buys a duck to save it from being killed and eaten. Now he has a problem. How can he keep his duck hidden inside his sports bag for several days?

And what's Grandad going to say when he brings the duck home to the flat?

Michael's *Out of the Ashes* is also closely linked to Nethercott and Iddesleigh. The book tells the story of a Devon farming family during the outbreak of Foot and Mouth Disease in 2001. Around Iddesleigh, the crisis was particularly severe – no one could ignore

the huge mounds of stiff, slaughtered cattle. Farmers could do nothing but watch as a life's work literally went up in plumes of thick, black smoke as the carcasses burned. The stench was sickening. Michael and Clare felt keenly for their friends and neighbours and decided that children throughout the United Kingdom ought to know more of this grim story. The book is dedicated to all those who suffered such hardship at that time.

In the early years at Nethercott, Michael usually wrote the first draft of a story during the school holidays, when he could concentrate for several hours at a time. His drafting and redrafting could be fitted in around the time he spent with the visiting children during term. At that time, Michael managed some-how to be at the farm for the early morning milking, nip home to write for an hour or two, and then walk back down to the farm to be with the children again around lunchtime. Then he was off home again and then back once more for evening milking. In later years, the farm was very well managed by other people, and Michael and Clare have now officially retired from their daily involvement with Farms for City Children. However, they still spend time there and Michael still reads or tells stories to the children every week if he possibly can. Michael and Clare also visit the other two farms and Michael gives talks around the country to help raise money for the project.

Around 3,000 children each year spend a week at the farms. Michael and Clare's work for Farms for City Children was recognised by the award of an MBE (Member of the British Empire) to each of them in 1999.

Clare and Michael receiving their MBEs at Buckingham Palace, October 1999.

Michael says he has slowed down, but he seems to be writing more than ever. When he became the Children's Laureate in 2003, his busy programme required him to travel all over the country giving talks in schools, attending meetings and speaking at conferences and festivals. Michael is the first to say that the farm, his writing, his talks and his work on committees have always been a two-person job. 'Clare runs my life', he says, for she keeps control of his crowded diary, makes and receives countless telephone calls, and types up his longhand manuscripts on the computer. (Michael and modern technology are not close friends.) Theirs is very much a partnership. Her views on everything from the plot of a story to the detailed arrangements for a speaking tour are always crucial. She is his first and best critic, whose advice is never ignored. Mostly, she keeps him sane too.

Michael was once asked in an on-line interview, 'If you did not have time for both, would you give up the farm or your writing?' He replied:

> I would not want to give up either, ever. But, if I'm frank, I think the writing would have to go. The welfare of the children who come to the farm is very important to me. So are the people who work with and for Farms for City Children … In a way, the farm is my best story.

Fortunately, he doesn't see the farm and his writing as separate areas of his life. To write well, he thinks, he needs to live a life crowded with interest and people – he isn't the kind of writer who can sit alone in a room writing all day long. To write well for children, he needs to spend time with them, listening to them, talking to them. Michael writes for children, rather than for adult readers, chiefly because he's always lived with children. First, he was a child himself, often surrounded by other boys at boarding school. Then he had his own children, then he taught children, then he lived and worked alongside children every day at the farm, and now he has six grandchildren. He has always been interested in the way children see the world, the kinds of questions they ask and the fact that they never stop asking them. 'I feel very lucky', he says. 'I don't particularly think that I am writing for young readers while I am actually writing a story – it's just that they are constantly a part of my life and that shapes the way I write.'

Although Iddesleigh is their very secure base, there are other places which have been special for the family – and sources for Michael's stories. Life at Nethercott coupled with Michael's writing and work in schools was sometimes *too* intense. The family needed to get away together from the farm, and to get away from the telephone and the morning pile of

Michael with HRH Princess Anne at Nethercott, 2003.

letters. For a while, the Morpurgos owned a holiday
cottage near Zennor in Cornwall. Then, more
importantly, there are the Scilly Isles. Michael and
his family have visited one of the islands, Bryher, for a
couple of weeks each summer for more than 25 years
– it was Horatio, the birdwatcher of the family, who
persuaded them to go there first, for the islands
attract large numbers of sea and coastal birds, some
of which are rarely seen elsewhere. Bryher offers a
change of pace – though even on holiday Michael
cannot help finding the seeds of a story. 'There's a
tale beneath every rock and wreck in the Scillies',
says Michael. *Why the Whales Came*, *The Wreck of the*

Children from Hoxton swimming in the
River Torridge, Nethercott, 1976.

Zanzibar, *Arthur, High King of Britain* and *The Sleeping Sword* are all set in the islands.

Michael and Clare's roots in Devon and the Scillies now run very deep and seem to sustain Michael's mind and imagination day by day. There's always something different to see in a stretch of countryside when you know it well. It changes with the weather, sometimes several times a day. A ring of feathers by the hedge will tell you that a sparrowhawk killed there a couple of hours ago. You can see where a badger has broken through a fence, even though you put a rock there to stop him only yesterday. And yet you know that this landscape, for all its daily changes, is also ancient. It was there long before you came and it will be there long after you have gone. For Michael, it's a good place for a writer to belong.

Where Do You Get Your
Ideas From, Mr Morpurgo?

Where Do You Get Your Ideas From, Mr Morpurgo?

Almost every time Michael gives a talk in a school, someone will ask that question. He always tries to answer, though he also insists there is something mysterious about the whole process of writing a story. What is more, if he tries to analyse how he writes too closely, he believes he runs the risk of losing some of the life at the heart of the story itself.

'Where do you get your ideas from?' may seem a simple question, but the trouble with simple questions is that they expect simple answers. It isn't that simple for Michael to explain where his ideas come from or, for that matter, how those ideas come together to make a story. The answers are about as complicated as the human mind's ability to connect two or three – or more – ideas which, at first, don't seem to have much to do with each other. Making such connections takes time, which is why Michael is astonished that children in school are expected to write complete stories in 45 minutes when they take tests. He couldn't manage that himself. For Michael, a story can be brewing in his mind for weeks, or months, or even longer before he is ready to start writing. He calls this period his 'dream-time'.

Here is one of Michael's attempts to answer *that* question, written in a magazine in 1993:

> A writer is a prospector. A prospector may find gold by accident or on purpose, by a mere glance at a glinting river-bed or by years of laborious back-aching panning. He may never find gold at all. What a prospector does with his gold is another matter. He could drink it, invest it, pawn it, or bury it.

Michael often says how lucky he has been – stories seem to fall into his path. But a prospector has to have a good eye for spotting a place where gold might be found, and Michael does have an excellent eye for spotting an idea which might one day be valuable in the making of a story.

He also talks about being a 'gatherer': someone who collects a snippet from a conversation here, a newspaper item there or maybe a few words over-heard on a train. Mostly, though, Michael 'gathers' from his own memories, and to have memories you have to live a life worth remembering. Hence the most important thing for him is to hunt out experiences, to visit interesting or unusual places, to listen and talk to children and adults. Many of his stories are about people who suffer some kind of hardship or are treated unfairly – even cruelly. Without being pompous or pious about it, he believes it is necessary for a writer to care about what happens to other people. To be a writer, he thinks, you also need curiosity – you have to go on asking *why*, just as small children never seem to stop asking why. 'You need', he says, 'to drink in the world around you.'

Quite often, in the evening, Michael jots down in his notebook two or three lines about the most memorable thing that's happened to him during the day. It might be a conversation he had in the pub, something he's seen on television or read in the paper. It might be something he's been told by one of the children at Nethercott or a pupil in a school he's visited. Some time later, often much later, those two or three lines may come in handy.

For Michael, it's sometimes a matter of trying to make connections; but more often, he has to wait to let connections happen. It's no good trying to force ideas together. And some ideas, of course, don't connect up with anything else – not for a while, anyway.

Michael also sees himself as a kind of weaver, taking strands which at first 'seem to be miles and miles apart' and eventually weaving them together into the whole tapestry of a story. This section is about the ideas and experiences that are woven together into some of Michael's best-known books. Each story grows through Michael's 'dream-time' – the period when ideas are stirring about in his mind, sometimes gently, sometimes so fiercely that he can't stop thinking about them: 'I dream my dream until it becomes so involving I can't stop dreaming it.'

When Michael has prospected for his ideas, gathered them together and woven them into the beginnings of the fabric of his story, the outline of his plot begins to emerge.

Then he faces the hard work of capturing the dream in writing and finding out exactly where his story is taking him.

War Horse (1982)

Michael's interest in war began when he was very young. His Uncle Peter had died wrestling with the controls of a badly damaged bomber, his Uncle Francis had led a cell of French Resistance fighters. He had often met his hero, the wounded Spitfire pilot, and much of the adult talk at home was about the war. Not surprisingly, Michael has always seized any opportunity to talk with old soldiers about their experiences and one evening in his village pub, the Duke of York, he found himself fascinated by the memories of an elderly villager who had fought in the First World War.

The old man had been little more than a boy when he had joined the Army. He was so used to working with horses on the land that he felt at home in a cavalry regiment, the Devon Yeomanry. Very soon, the excitement of being in uniform and going off to fight for king and country gave way to the harsh truth of what he and his friends would have to do on the battlefield. They were expected to ride their horses in a hell-for-leather charge across no man's land towards the German machine-guns and, if they were unlucky, the new-fangled armoured tanks. What chance would he and his horse stand? Riding a flesh-and-blood animal towards those machine-guns and tanks made no sense to anyone, except to the old generals who made the tactical decisions; and *their* tactics were based on the wars they had fought as young men when horses had been all-important on the battlefield.

The young farm boy was terrified when he thought of those cavalry charges. Even as he talked to Michael, 60 years later, the old soldier's eyes moistened into tears as he remembered friends who never returned to their Devon villages. Out there on the front line, never knowing if he would survive the next day's charge, he couldn't talk to anyone about his terror. All his mates were just as frightened as he was and talking to each other about their fears only made things worse. So, each night, he would go to the lines where the horses were tethered and talk quietly to the one friend he could confide in – the horse who would carry him next morning towards those machine-guns and tanks.

As the veteran soldier remembered those one-sided conversations long ago, Michael thought suddenly of a boy who had spent a week recently at Nethercott.

He was very shy and often stuttered badly when he talked to strangers – especially in front of other children. Michael remembered how he too used to stutter when asked to read aloud in class at his prep school. One November evening, Michael had gone into the stable yard at Nethercott and, unnoticed in the shadows, had overheard the boy talking – with no trace of a stutter at all – to one of the horses, telling her in great detail about everything he had been doing that day on the farm.

Michael listened to the old soldier's memories late into the evening and found himself deeply moved – and excited. Some days later, those memories connected with a memory of his own. When his father-in-law died, Michael had found among his books a number of original illustrations drawn for the *Illustrated London News* during the First World War. This weekly magazine regularly featured drawings by war artists, depicting thrilling scenes from the front line for readers at home. Usually, the British were shown triumphing yet again over the Germans, but one particular image had etched itself on Michael's memory. The British cavalry were charging at full gallop up a hillside towards some woods. Rolls of sharp barbed wire at the edge of the trees lay in wait for the riders and their horses. The German machine-gunners were entrenched behind the wire. Already, some horses and their riders lay on the hillside, mown down by the machine-guns; others writhed in the entangling wire, at the mercy of the enemy.

Michael had been horrified by the artist's image, but also fascinated. He began to read more widely about the use of horses in the Great War, as it is sometimes called. He came across a chilling statistic. One million British soldiers died on the battlefields of the First World War; but *two* million horses were blown to pieces, drowned in the mud or died from disease. No doubt, similar numbers of animals were lost by the French and German armies. When the war was finally won, the British government decided that it was too expensive to bring the surviving horses back across the channel from France. The Army sold the horses off to French butchers, to be served up on the dinner table. Michael was astonished and angered by this heartless reward for animals who had obediently done everything asked of them throughout a gruelling war.

The old soldier's memories, the boy in the Nethercott stable yard, the artist's impression of the cavalry charge and those two million horses; Michael's story of a Devon farm boy and his horse was taking shape. Now he felt passionately that he wanted his young readers to know that it was not only British soldiers and their horses who had endured such misery. How could he show the suffering of the people and animals of France, Belgium and Germany as well? Well, if a horse rather than a soldier were at the centre of his story, and if that horse were to find himself passed from owner to owner through the fortunes of war, from one side to the other, that might do it. Only the horse would know the whole story – the adventures, the hardships, the cruelties and the kindness to be found on both sides. His horse must tell the story himself. He'd call him 'Joey'.

*   *   *

Joey's story begins on a Devon farm close to a village very like Michael's own. From there, Joey's journey takes him through Army training and then over the Channel to the terrifying battlefields and trenches of Flanders. Joey and his friend, Topthorn, another cavalry horse, are captured and put to work pulling an ammunition cart driven by Friedrich, a gentle German whose 'whole nature cried out against fighting a war'. This extract describes the capture of the horses and their riders, Trooper Warren and Captain Stewart; Michael's use of the artist's drawing for the *Illustrated London News* is clearly evident:

> On my back, Trooper Warren held me in an iron grip with his knees, I stumbled once and felt him lose a stirrup, and slowed so that he could find it again. Topthorn was still ahead of me, his head up, his tail whisking from side to side. I found more strength

in my legs and charged after him. Trooper Warren prayed aloud as he rode, but his prayers soon turned to curses as he saw the carnage around him. Only a few horses reached the wire and Topthorn and I were amongst them. There were indeed a few holes blasted through the wire by our bombardment so that some of us could find a way through; and we came at last upon the first line of enemy trenches, but they were empty.

The firing came now from higher up in amongst the trees; and so the squadron, or what was left of it, regrouped and galloped up into the wood, only to be met by a line of hidden wire in amongst the trees. Some of the horses ran into the wire before they could be stopped, and stuck there, their riders trying feverishly to extract them. I saw one trooper dismount deliberately once he saw his horse was caught.

He pulled out his rifle and shot his mount before falling dead himself on the wire. I could see at once that the only way was to jump the wire and when I saw Topthorn and Captain Stewart leap over where the wire was lowest, I followed them and we found ourselves at last in amongst the enemy. From behind every tree, from trenches all around it seemed, they ran forward in their piked helmets to counter-attack. They rushed past us, ignoring us until we found ourselves surrounded by an entire company of soldiers, their rifles pointing up at us.

Why the Whales Came (1985)

Michael and his family were spending their first holiday on the Scilly Isles, which lie some 25 miles off the 'toe' of Cornwall. They were staying on Bryher, an island in the north-west corner of the little archipelago. To the south of Bryher is Samson. The map shows no roads on Samson; in fact, no people have lived there since the early years of the 20th century.

Michael needed a few hours away from his family to work on a book he was close to finishing. Samson promised to be ideal – all the peace and quiet he could wish. One morning, a fisherman from Bryher took him over to Samson by small boat. Even experienced writers are easily tempted to avoid getting down to work and here was an uninhabited island just asking to be explored. Michael decided he'd walk round the coastline – it wouldn't take long; *then* he'd start writing. Soon, he came across a cluster of fourteen ruined cottages. Signs of habitation still lay on the earth floors: a broken clay pipe, half the sole of a shoe and some piles of limpet shells, a reminder of one of the staple foods of the islanders when times were hard. As Michael went in and out of the cottages, he suddenly had a sense that he was not alone, a feeling that grew stronger as daylight began to fade.

Things weren't going as he had planned. The weather was rapidly changing, as it often does on the Scillies. The sky was growing darker by the minute and the white horses riding the crests of the waves told him that the sea was already too rough for the boatman from Bryher to pick him up. He was stranded. He spent the day drinking in the atmosphere of the island, more and more aware that the smoker of that clay pipe, the owner of that shoe and those who had survived on the limpets must have lived at the daily mercy of sea, wind and rain. If the storms raged for days on end, fishing would be impossible and food would soon be scarce. The story he had taken with him was no closer to getting finished; but he had begun to dream another one.

When he was finally able to return to Bryher late in the evening, Michael talked to the lady who owned the cottage in which the Morpurgos were staying. 'You've been on Samson? We don't go there – or, if we have to, never at night-time. It's haunted.' She told Michael about the last people who had lived on Samson, 60 or 70 years before. There'd been a terrible tragedy – a shipwreck when many of the men from the island had been drowned. The worst thing was that it had been completely unnecessary – she couldn't remember the details, but it had been greed which drove the men to put to sea. The islanders who were left, mostly women and children, could no longer survive on Samson and were forced to leave. One old woman refused to go. Like the Birdman's mother in *Why the Whales Came*, she stayed on until she died.

Michael needed a similar tragedy to threaten the islanders in the story which was beginning to emerge in his mind. But what kind of tragedy? The answer came in a book he was given by his son Horatio, a keen wildlife enthusiast. One of the chapters told how a couple of narwhals – whales with horns two or even three metres long – had come up the Thames and been found beached, with their heads cut off. Someone wanted those horns for the high price they would fetch. At the conclusion of Michael's novel, the young hero and heroine stand with their friend the Birdman against all the other islanders, protecting a stranded narwhal. The islanders want it for its meat and the money they'll get for its horn. What is even worse, just out in the bay there is a huge shoal of narwhals, trying to come ashore themselves, as if to help their stranded friend. The people of the island foresee huge riches if they get their hands on the horns. The three friends are determined to save the animals from slaughter. Michael had the seeds of the tragedy he was looking for – three against many, courage against greed, the deaths of those mysterious and beautiful creatures … He could make something of that!

*   *   *

Why the Whales Came is one of Michael's most successful novels; it has also been made into a feature film and a stage play.

Gracie Jenkins, the heroine of the story, was about ten years old in 1914. The First World War broke out that year and although the fighting in Europe seemed far distant from the peaceful islands, the war touched the lives of even the children of Bryher.

Now, around 70 years later, Gracie tells her story. It begins with her friendship with Daniel, the son of a local boat builder. Gracie and Daniel are boat-builders of a kind too, and they love to sail the model boats they make. When a pair of nesting swans occupies their favourite pool, they take their boats over to the outer shore of Bryher.

Gracie and Daniel are now in forbidden territory. The west coast, with the great Atlantic waves crashing onto the wild beaches, was too dangerous for children. Even more frightening, this was where the mysterious Birdman of Bryher lived among the dunes. Gracie and Daniel become friends of the strange old man, cloaked in his black cape, a fierce one-legged kittiwake perched on his shoulder.

Gracie's story tells of prejudice and bullying, a dangerous adventure adrift in a fog, a night in the haunted village on Samson and an anxious struggle to rescue a stranded narwhal.

Michael's experience alone on Samson is also the source for his short story, 'The Story That Wrote Itself', which appears on page 239 of this book.

Waiting for Anya (1990) and *The Dancing Bear* (1994)

Clare and Michael had attended a wedding in south-west France – the marriage of their son Sebastian and his French bride. After the celebrations, they took the chance of a few days' exploration of the Pyrenees, the mountains which form the border between France and Spain. Michael rather fancied being photographed against a background of mountains, standing with one foot in France and one in Spain.

On the advice of their new in-laws, Michael and Clare set off for Lescun, a village perched high on a mountainside, not far from the border. They missed the turning for the road which winds up the hairpin bends to Lescun and, instead, they found themselves approaching the small village of Borce. Beside the road, Clare spotted an intriguing sign – a picture of a bear above an arrow pointing off the main road and through the village. That looked promising, and an arrow pointing somewhere – anywhere – was helpful, since they were lost. Borce turned out to be nothing special, but beyond its old church Michael and Clare found, with the help of another bear-and-arrow sign, a large cage with a melancholy bear sitting inside. A notice in large print told them that this was Jojo, a European bear.

In smaller print, they read the story of how Jojo came to be there. One day some fourteen years earlier, a young boy from the village had been playing by a stream when he felt a gentle, almost playful, nudge on the back of his neck. It was a bear cub. Any sighting of bears was unusual since they had been hunted close to extinction and man had encroached more and more on the animals' terri-tories. The villagers fed and cared for the cub – they guessed that an adult bear that had been shot recently must have been the mother. In time, Jojo grew too large to be allowed to wander round the village – which explained the cage. He became a rather sad tourist attraction; sales of local honey, in jars decor-ated with a special bear label, went up sharply.

Michael and Clare got directions in Borce and before long found the road up to Lescun, where they knew there was a hotel. The first thing they saw in the hotel lobby was a bearskin hanging on the wall, close to a black-and-white photograph of a bear hunt around 1940. 'I was beginning to tingle. Wild horses would not have driven me away', says Michael. He and Clare booked a room.

Over the next few days, Michael and Clare explored some of the paths which led up from the village towards the peaks. On one walk, a huge white Pyrenean mountain dog – he was almost as big as a Shetland pony – insisted on coming along with them. High in the pastures above Lescun, they found a shepherd. Every summer since he was sixteen, he'd lived up in the mountains in his hut, milking his sheep and making cheese. Once a week, he would load up his donkey and bring his cheeses down to the village. Clare duly photographed Michael standing in France and Spain at the same time, and they walked

Michael at Lescun.

back down to Lescun, the white dog still keeping them company.

That night, Michael lay in bed and began to dream his story. A shepherd, a bear, jars of honey, sheep's cheese, the border and a Pyrenean mountain dog might all come into it somehow. Time to ask some questions.

Next day, he spoke with some of the village people. No, they no longer shot bears. Michael asked what happened during the Second World War. They'd been occupied by German troops. In spite of the German soldiers, the paths from the village up to the mountain pass and over into neutral Spain had been used by Allied aircrew who had been shot down but avoided being captured. Groups of Jews and other refugees had gone that way too, escaping probable death in the Nazi concentration camps. Michael chatted to the former mayor of the village – he'd been a boy in Lescun during the war. Yes, he remembered the Germans – they'd not been a bad lot. Many of them were older men, not fit enough for front-line fighting – some had even fought in the First World War and hated this new war as much as the villagers did. They kept themselves to themselves, as did the villagers. Michael asked the mayor about a cross he'd noticed on a hairpin bend below the village. The mayor avoided the question, so, thought Michael, there must be a story of some kind there – something the village would rather forget. That could be useful for *his* story.

When Michael and Clare returned to their new French in-laws, Michael asked more questions, for some of the family were old enough to remember the German occupation. He heard stories of how French Jews had been rounded up and sent off to the death camps – some had been packed off like cattle in trains to Auschwitz or Bergen Belsen, but others had been sent to a camp at Gurs, only a few kilometres away. Michael visited the site of the camp and, he recalls, 'I saw the gravestones and wept inside.'

For a year, he dreamed the dream of this new story, everything he had discovered on his visit shifting around in his mind. He read a good deal. He talked with other French friends. Then his story was ready to be written.

* * *

Waiting for Anya is set in Lescun during the German occupation. Several escaping Jewish children have gathered in the village after their journey along the 'underground railway', the secret routes through France used by refugees, unknown to the German troops. In Lescun, the children are hidden in the barn of the Widow Horcada (a name Michael found on the village war memorial). The problem is, how can the children be moved out of the village up to the mountain passes on their way to Spain without arousing the suspicion of the Germans?

Eventually, the villagers work together to trick the Germans by inviting them to an organ concert in the village church. The Germans politely accept, only to find that the concert goes on and on – and on – until the refugees have all been shepherded out of the village and off up the path. As in *War Horse*, Michael shows how many of the German soldiers are caught up in a war they hate. One of them is a veteran of the Battle of Verdun in 1916, which lasted for ten months with hundreds of thousands of casualties on both sides. The old soldier forges a strong bond with the story's central character, Jo, for both are birdwatchers, delighting especially in the soaring flight of a pair of eagles. The timeless mountains are almost characters in the story themselves; they contrast with the brutal yet trivial nature of warfare. Michael is especially pleased this book is very popular in its French translation, which is simply entitled *Anna*.

Michael had not finished with his visit to the mountains yet, for in 1994 he published *The Dancing Bear*, which drew directly on his memories of what he called 'that raggedy old bear' in the cage at Borce and the consequent increase in the sales of honey. Here, an orphan bear cub is cared for by an equally lonely orphan girl, Roxanne. All seems well at first, for both the cub and Roxanne, now inseparable, feel secure in the affection the whole village seems to feel for them. But then, the peaceful mountain world is turned upside down by the arrival of a film crew and the glamorous celebrity, Niki. And, to make his latest promotional video, Niki needs a dancing bear ...

The War of Jenkins' Ear (1993)

Michael's painful memories of his prep school are still sharp: the miserable journey to school from Victoria Station at the start of every term, the homesickness, the bullying, the canings, the fear of getting answers wrong in class. Like the school he later wrote about in *The Butterfly Lion*, 'it was a diet of Latin and stew and rugby and cross-country runs and chilblains and marks and squeaky beds and semolina pudding'. Or, as he calls it later in the same story, *slimey* semolina pudding.

Looking back as an adult on those unhappy days at school, Michael also recalls the way everyone at the school seemed to despise the children who lived beyond the school gates in the local village. Even the masters told their pupils, 'We don't want you behaving like those village boys.' Michael and his friends called the village children 'oiks'. The prep school boys believed that the oiks were nowhere near as intelligent and nowhere near as good at games as they were – in fact, nowhere near as good. *They* weren't like *us*. If you don't know people, you are often scared of them. When the boys from Michael's school left the safety of the school grounds and trotted through the village on cross-country runs every Tuesday afternoon, they were always anxious in case they met the villagers. When they did, stones as well as insults were sometimes hurled by both sides.

This feud seemed all wrong to one of the boys at Michael's school. He was older than Michael and he had a kind of magnetism which drew Michael and one or two other boys towards him. Together, they made a small camp – a kind of den – hidden in the undergrowth in the school grounds where they could meet and talk in secret. Here, the older boy told his young disciples that holy voices had spoken to him, commanding him to put an end to the enmity between the prep school boys and the villagers. He tried to stop the violence and the feuding by preaching to the other boys. In his own eyes, in fact, he was not merely a preacher. He believed that his voices told him that he was the next Jesus Christ, fulfilling the Bible's prophecy that Jesus would one day return to earth. And Michael, for a while, was so impressed that he believed him.

Somehow, the Headmaster got to hear that a pupil

was claiming to be Jesus Christ. This was not only serious, it was blasphemous. What if the parents got to hear of this? In morning assembly, the Head talked to the whole school about what he had heard. Any boy who knew anything about this should stand up. Michael felt that in some way he ought to support his friend, but he couldn't see what he could do. He felt like Judas who betrayed Christ – or Simon Peter who denied knowing Jesus before the crucifixion.

The War of Jenkins' Ear is probably Michael's most autobiographical book. If you read it alongside *The Butterfly Lion* and the short story called 'My One and Only Great Escape' in *Ten of the Best*, you will have a strong picture of the most difficult and dramatic elements of Michael's early schooldays.

* * *

Toby, who tells the story, is caught in the middle of the class war between the private school boys and the village children. The hatred between the two groups and their fear of each other run deep, as this extract shows when the prep school boys face their enemies across the river that marks the boundary of the school grounds:

The chant around Toby was a murmur at first, then it became rhythmic and swelled. 'Oik, oik, oik, oik. Oik,

oik, oik, oik.' The crescendo built slowly, and from the other side came the reply: 'Toff, toff, toff, toff. Toff, toff, toff, toff.' Toby looked around him, at the faces of his friends. They were contorted with fury, their eyes blazing, their feet stamping, their fists punching the air and he noticed that many of the fists held stones.

Only Christopher, a new boy, stands out against this warfare – like the boy who so impressed Michael when he was at prep school, he hears voices and believes himself to be the Christ. Toby meanwhile is trapped in the very masculine, enclosed society of the school. Much of the time he is anxious and frightened, in class and out, despite his success on the rugby field and in the school choir. Just like Michael, Toby desperately wants to make his father proud of him – but whatever he does, it never seems to be enough. And, just like Michael again, Toby has to decide whether to stand by Christopher or to betray him. As Michael sees it, the novel is not only about the conflict between different social classes; it is also about the difference between faith and superstition.

Arthur, High King of Britain
(1994)

Michael's love of old tales of heroes and heroines has led him to retell some of the stories for young readers today, such as *Robin of Sherwood* and *Joan of Arc*. His retelling of his favourite, *Sir Gawain and the Green Knight*, was published in 2004. Ten years earlier, he wrote a collection of stories about King Arthur and his Knights of the Round Table which appeared in a handsome book with illustrations by Michael Foreman.

Michael feels the original versions of these old legends are usually much tougher than those often found in books and films today. *Robin Hood* should be about poverty, revolution and treachery, not about the jolly life of singing and feasting in the greenwood – with a bit of archery and swordplay thrown in. Looking back, he thinks one of the reasons he loved *Sir Gawain* at university was that it was about a real human being who knew fear and temptation; Gawain was not at all like, say, Sir Galahad, who is often one of the main characters in versions written for children. 'He's too good to be true', thinks Michael. 'He's so *boring*.'

Almost 150 years before Michael wrote *Arthur, High King of Britain*, another writer had been looking for a way to tell *his* generation the stories of the Arthurian legend. In 1850, Alfred, Lord Tennyson, had been appointed Poet Laureate. The Poet Laureate's task is to celebrate the national triumphs and events of his age, and in the time of Queen Victoria, the people of Britain believed there were plenty of national triumphs and events worth celebrating. But Tennyson also wanted to write about Britain's *past* glories, including the ancient tales of King Arthur and his Knights of the Round Table. Just as Michael spends time exploring an area where he plans to set a story, Tennyson hoped to find a place where Arthur might have fought his final, fatal battle against his own illegitimate son, Mordred.

Cornwall seemed a likely place to look, since the castle at Tintagel on the cliffs of the north coast features in some versions of the Arthurian stories. So Tennyson set off with his friend, Holman Hunt, who painted several pictures based upon Tennyson's poems. Eventually, not far from Land's End, close to the tip of the Cornish peninsula, the two men found a likely beach. Here was a freshwater lake lying behind the dunes – just the place for Sir Bedevere to hurl

Arthur's great sword, Excalibur, out over the water where a magical hand in a silken sleeve rose from the depths to seize it. There was even a mound nearby where Tennyson could visualise Arthur and Mordred locked in a combat ended only by Mordred's treacherous blow. Here too the boat carrying Arthur to his last resting place might be launched.

Tennyson and Hunt stood together, gazing out to sea. Where could that last resting place for Arthur be? The legend said that here the king would lie in a sleep of seeming death, waiting to answer his country's call in time of need once more.

The poet wondered aloud what lay far out to the west, beyond the horizon.

'America', said Holman Hunt.

'Nothing else until you reach America?'

'Only the Scilly Isles.'

The next day, Tennyson and Hunt boarded the little packet boat that sailed regularly between Penzance and the Scillies. In Tregarthen's Hotel on St Mary's, Michael discovered a small plaque recording 'Alfred, Lord Tennyson, stayed here'. Somewhere on these islands, the most westerly point of England, Tennyson had decided, was the place where Arthur should lie in his long sleep.

If the Scillies were good enough for a Poet Laureate, thought Michael, they would serve for him too. He wanted to know exactly where Arthur was resting and waiting in *his* story, since Michael loves the idea of linking the present to the past through a single place. In Michael's *Robin of Sherwood*, an old oak tree in the forest comes crashing down in a gale. Within the crater left by its torn roots, a boy from our time finds an arrowhead, a horn and a skull, and he also finds a way through into Robin Hood's time. On the Scillies, Michael wanted a place for his hero

Arthur.

to gain entrance into Arthur's time to find the
resting king.

Michael spread his map of the Scillies out on the
bed.

'Where do you think he should be buried – which
island?' he asked Clare.

She was used to such questions but she couldn't
honestly see that it made much difference.

'Of course it does', said Michael. 'We've got to get it *right*.'

'Oh, very well', said Clare, 'He was buried … *there*!'

Her finger landed on the map within a centimetre of a tiny uninhabited island – there are dozens like it in the Scillies. This one, the map told them, was called Little Arthur. Perfect!

It wasn't too difficult for Michael to find his story of the boy from our time who was to discover Arthur in his cave beneath the rocky outcrops of the islands. There, from Arthur's own lips, he would hear the great tales of Sir Lancelot, Sir Gawain, Sir Tristram and the rest. Michael already knew from his holidays on the Scillies that the islanders claim that in certain conditions you could walk, or maybe run, right around the outer islands when the tide was out without getting your feet too wet. Maybe you'd have to do a bit of wading here and there. Michael thought his young hero might set out to see if it really could be done. Then, somehow, he'd get into difficulties. And then … ?

Well, then there was the old Scillies story of the mysterious bell which, fishermen swear, you could hear tolling through the fog when conditions were very bad. Sometimes, it even seemed to come from under the sea. His wandering boy might follow the sound of the bell, trusting it to guide him to safety. At times the bell would seem close at hand, at times far away. His boy would have no choice but to follow, even when he was caught by fierce currents and dragged down into the cold of the sea. And when he woke … he'd find himself in a great bed covered with skins, watched over by a huge friendly dog and an old man in a long grey cloak. And then …

All this and that lucky finger landing right beside Little Arthur too. It was time for Michael to start writing.

The Wreck of the Zanzibar
(1995)

Samson may be haunted, but it's been a lucky island for Michael. Not only did he find the seeds of the story of *Why the Whales Came* on Samson, but on a later visit he discovered a leather-backed turtle washed up on the shore. That turtle set him off on the journey that led to *The Wreck of the Zanzibar*, winner of the Whitbread Children's Novel Award in 1996.

Michael was fascinated as he crouched beside the turtle's head. Just like the face of a little wrinkled old man, he thought. Or ET maybe. The turtle's eyes were open wide in death and Michael stared deep into them. 'How far have you come, eh? What happened to you – what's your story?' he wondered. As he gazed into the mysteries of those eyes, Michael already sensed that there was a story here, waiting to be explored.

Michael knew nothing about leather-backed turtles. His research soon taught him that they were strangers in the Scillies. Their homes are thousands of miles away in the warm southern seas. Their favourite food is jellyfish and sometimes the turtles will follow their prey far out into the great oceans. Storms may scatter the shoals of jellyfish and Michael's turtle might have been caught up in powerful currents, sweeping it ever further from its home. Maybe it had been injured in a collision with a passing boat, maybe it had been weakened by the chill of alien waters and finally been stranded on this beach in the Scillies to die.

So there was to be a turtle in his story, Michael knew. But what else? Nothing much came to mind at first, but now he was definitely on the lookout. Later on that same holiday, Michael noticed a fine old black-and-white photograph displayed in a shop window on St Mary's, the largest of the islands. The photographers, Alexander and Herbert Gibson, were famous for their pictures of life on the Scillies in the early years of the 20th century, especially of ships wrecked on the rocky coasts. This photograph showed one of the island gigs, stern sail set, the crew of eight men bending to the oars, ploughing through heavy seas on their way out to a wrecked vessel.

Getting to a wreck was a matter of urgency. When a ship foundered on the rocks, the islanders did every-thing they could to rescue the crew first, of course. Then the tradition was that anything they could salvage from the ship's cargo or the timbers of the ship itself belonged to them, although sometimes the customs officers tried to prevent them. When a boat ran aground, the gigs from nearby islands would race each other to try to gain the prize of the valuable salvage. Even in the 1990s, when a container ship carrying 10,000 pairs of Reeboks was wrecked, everyone on the islands seemed somehow to have acquired new trainers and a few pairs to spare.

Michael asked the shopkeeper if he knew the story behind the photograph. 'That's the gig from Bryher, on her way out to the wreck of the *Minnehaha* in 1910', the shopkeeper told him. The *Minnehaha* was a fortunate wreck for the islanders; there had been cows on board and the islanders had managed to lasso them and bring them safely ashore. Those cows had established a new herd on Bryher.

Michael felt he had almost found his story. He still needed something to 'open it up', much as you might need a key to open up a treasure chest. Some more time dreaming the story in his head went by. He kept on asking questions. He knew that Scillies gigs still existed – in fact they were still raced, every Friday evening in the summer, largely for the benefit of the tourists. 'Do women – or girls – ever row in the gigs?' he asked a local friend one day. 'They never used to – it was a men-only affair. But just recently, they've let one or two row in the crews.'

'And there', says Michael, 'I'd found my little key.'

Michael and Clare on a visit to the Scilly Isles, 1990.

*   *   *

The turtle, a wreck, the rescued cows, a girl in the gig – they all are woven together to make the fabric of *The Wreck of the Zanzibar*, told by 14-year-old Laura Perryman in her diary for 1907. She longs to row

119

alongside her father and her twin brother Billy in the Bryher gig, but she's firmly told that this is man's work. Times are hard and Billy is tired of working every hour of the day on the family farm, tired of constant rows with his father and tired of life on the islands. So he runs away to seek his fortune aboard an American schooner, the *General Lee*. How Laura is desperately needed to row in the gig, how the sailors of the *Zanzibar* are rescued, how some cows are brought ashore just in time to save the livelihood of Laura's family – that's the story Michael tells. As for that leather-backed turtle who started it all – we find out why, almost 100 years after Laura's adventure, a large wooden turtle often plays an important part in the games of the children of Bryher.

The Butterfly Lion (1996)

The *Butterfly Lion* began, you could say, when Michael fell in love. He was only ten at the time, but it was important. The lady in question was Virginia McKenna, who was more than twice Michael's age. Sadly, he had met her only on the cinema screen in films like *Carve Her Name with Pride* in which she had played Violette Szabo, an agent in the French Resistance who was eventually captured, interrogated and shot, but she never betrayed her friends in the Resistance. Michael had also seen her in *The Cruel Sea*, a wartime naval drama in which she had appeared in uniform; she looked terrific. Virginia McKenna had the kind of cool beauty which her fans at the time used to compare to an English rose. Even more important, as Michael and thousands of other movie-going schoolboys of the 1950s knew, she was just the kind of woman a chap needed beside him when he was busy dreaming of winning the Second World War all over again.

One day, 40 years or more after his emotionally unsettling encounter in the cinema, Michael met Virginia McKenna again, this time in a lift in a Dublin hotel. He had just been speaking at a conference and he was now heading for his hotel room to collect his suitcase on his way to the airport. And there he was, alone in a lift with – it really was her, wasn't it? – Virginia McKenna. He just *had* to say something. But what? If he didn't speak soon, it could be too late – she might get out at the next floor and the moment would be gone for ever, never to return. He would regret it for the rest of his life.

Quick thinking as ever, Michael decided it was too late to tell her how he had felt about her when he was ten. He also remembered seeing her in a film called *Born Free* with her husband, Bill Travers, which focused on a family of lions in Africa. He knew that since they had made the movie, Virginia McKenna and her husband had done a great deal of charitable work for wild animals so – it was now or never – he said, 'Excuse me, but I just wanted to say how much I admired the work you and your husband have done through your Born Free Foundation. I think it's wonderful.'

She smiled as only Virginia McKenna could smile and said something along the lines of 'That's very sweet of you', and then it was all over almost before it had begun. The lift stopped, the doors opened, and she was gone. Back in his room, Michael felt foolish and ridiculous at the same time. 'What a stupid thing to say! What an idiot she must have thought me!' he thought. 'Still, too late now.'

He was just packing a few copies of his books into his suitcase when he suddenly knew what he could do. He wrote a note to Virginia McKenna on the title page of a copy of *The Dancing Bear*. After all, she was very concerned about caged animals, he knew that. When he was leaving the hotel, he left the book at the reception desk for her.

As you would expect, Virginia McKenna replies to her fans just as faithfully as Michael does himself. About a week later, Michael received a letter, thanking him for the book which, she said, she had much enjoyed. It just happened that Michael was thinking of writing a story about a lion – a white lion. Not long before his trip to Dublin, he had been on a train en route from London to Exeter. On the journey, he was enjoying a book called *The White Lions of Timbavati* by Chris McBride. There was a photograph of two white lion cubs on the cover. Then the train came to a stop, a few miles outside Westbury, right beside a hillside in Wiltshire which most people who use that route look out for. Carved into the chalky hillside there is a huge white horse. So, thought Michael, if you can have a white horse, why not a white *lion*? No reason at all. Clever idea, Morpurgo –

hold on to it. But *why* would anyone carve a white lion on a hillside?

Nothing had come of his bright idea – not until his meeting with Virginia McKenna and her letter got him thinking about lions again. Why *would* anyone carve a white lion on a hillside? Well, there was a true story that Michael had heard about a soldier in the First World War who rescued some circus animals in France from certain death – surely there'd have to be a lion among them. Michael had wanted to use this incident somehow. Maybe he could invent a reason for carving that white lion on the hillside that connected with the soldier and the circus animals?

What he needed was a narrative to join the different threads, though. And he had to find a role for a young hero or heroine as his central character. There was something else Michael had been wanting to write about – that time when he had run away from his prep school and been persuaded to go back by an elderly lady who had fed him tea and sympathy. She had even dropped him off by a hole in the hedge so that he wouldn't be spotted walking up the main school drive.

Virginia McKenna was able to give Michael a good deal of help about lions in captivity and in the wild in Africa. She was delighted when *The Butterfly Lion* was published. The book is dedicated to her and she has become a loyal supporter of various projects in which

Michael is involved, much to his pleasure. She sometimes attends productions of plays based on his novels on the London stage. When an audiotaped version of *The Butterfly Lion* was made, she played the part of the elderly lady who tells the runaway pupil the story of how a white lion came to be carved on a hillside near her home, whilst Michael himself read the rest of the narrative.

Farm Boy (1997)

Farm Boy is probably Michael's favourite book. Like *The Rainbow Bear* and *Billy the Kid*, it began with a suggestion by his friend, Michael Foreman, who has illustrated many of Michael's stories. ('I think he gets ideas for what he would like to illustrate and then he flatters me into writing the stories', says Michael.) Michael Foreman wanted a story that gave him a chance to show how life on the farm *used* to be.

Farm Boy also grew from the many letters Michael received from readers demanding to know what happened to Joey, the hero of *War Horse*, when he came back to Iddesleigh with 'the Corporal', the soldier who had spent all his pay to save him from the horse-butchers.

Michael's daughter Rosalind was very helpful in the writing of *Farm Boy*. She used to talk with Michael about her work with adults who, for various reasons, had never learned to read or write. In their conversations, Michael found an idea which is at the centre of *Farm Boy*. The story is told by a boy who spends his school holidays on a farm near Iddesleigh with his Grandpa – 'the only person I've ever met who seems utterly contented with his own place on earth, with the life he's lived'. One day, though, Grandpa confesses that he has never learned to read and write. He missed a year's schooling through being off with scarlet fever; in any case, he liked helping his father on the farm too much, and at times like harvest his help was much needed. 'You ask me where I'd rather be, in Mr Burton's writing lesson at school, or cleaning out the pigs? Pigs any day.'

Late in life, Grandpa sees how good it would be to be able to read his favourite Agatha Christie and Sherlock Holmes detective stories for himself – he's only been able to see them in their television versions.

Eventually, thanks to his grandson's teaching, he learns not only to read but to write the story of what happened when his own father, 'the Corporal' of *War Horse*, came back to Devon with Joey.

Michael's old friend Sean Rafferty provided much of the character for Grandpa – even 'Burrow', the cottage where Grandpa lives is based on Sean Rafferty's home. Sean was far from being unable to read and write. He was a fine poet, though not much interested in getting his work published; he wrote because he had something to say, and that was enough. He was also a wonderful conversationalist with a great sense of humour. Sean lived very simply – he was very securely rooted in his friendships and in the natural world around him. He was at ease with himself – and that is the way in which he was the model for Grandpa in the story.

Kensuke's Kingdom (1982)

Kensuke's Kingdom is Michael's best-selling book to date. It began with a request. Or rather, a command.

Opening the post over breakfast one morning, Michael found a letter from a boy. Nothing surprising in that, since he gets fifteen or twenty letters from fans most days. This one started rather unusually, though:

> Dear Mr Morpingo,
> I have just read your book *The Wreck of the Zanzibar*. It's the best book I have ever read. It is miles better than any Harry Potter book.

Michael decided he rather liked this particular correspondent. He clearly had excellent judgement. He read on.

> BUT, there's one thing definitely wrong with this book. It's about a girl. Write me a book about a boy who gets stuck on a desert island.

That was it. No messing about. No 'please'. Just get on with it, Mr Morpingo. Michael never throws suggestions away; at least, not for a few minutes.

'What do you think?' he asked Clare. 'Boy stuck on a desert island? Could be good, eh?'

'No it couldn't', said Clare firmly. 'It's been done before, and rather well done too. Remember? *Robinson Crusoe*? *Lord of the Flies*? *Coral Island*? And just a few others as well.'

Even though Michael always listens to Clare's advice, the idea didn't quite go away. Some ideas insist on hanging around in his mind for a few days, and this one did. The trouble was that Michael couldn't see how he could strand a boy on an island in a way that hadn't been done before. Couldn't do a plane crash – that was *Lord of the Flies*. Couldn't do pirates – that was *Treasure Island*. Most of the others were shipwrecks. It looked as though this particular idea was going to be filed in the waste-paper basket.

Then, one evening, Michael and Clare were guests at a neighbour's drinks party. Michael is quickly bored at the best of times, and parties where you stand around sipping a drink and talking to people you hardly know and will never meet again are, for him, the worst of times. He was being polite and smiling a lot, but still trying to catch Clare's eye so that they could fade quietly away home without anyone noticing. Another guest – who was probably just as bored as Michael – began chatting to him. For want of something better to talk about, Michael asked him what he did for a living.

'Nothing much, right now. I've just come back from sailing round the world on a yacht, actually.'

Michael's storyteller's antennae twitched. Yachts? Desert islands, maybe?

'Really – how did you come to do that?'

'I'd lost my job, you see, and I was wandering around the house all day doing nothing and getting more and more depressed. Being a bit of a pain, I suppose. So my wife said I had to *do* something.'

The man had done something. He sold the family car and the house, bought a yacht and set off round the world with his wife, their son and the family dog.

The boy stuck on the desert island in the back of Michael's mind was showing definite signs of life. A family sailing round the world. One little accident and the boy could be overboard and washed up on the island. That might work.

A little later, Michael came across an article in a magazine about dogs on sailing vessels – the writer mentioned how dogs could be attached to safety harnesses in rough weather to prevent them being swept overboard. If someone forgot to attach the dog – and for some reason the yacht lurched suddenly – the boy and the dog might both be tipped overboard – and the dog could end up on the island with the boy.

Michael saw that he'd need to know much more about long distance sailing if he was going to make the journey convincing. Practical research is often very important for the kinds of books Michael writes, so this time he signed up for a sailing course. He learned a good deal at first-hand about being seasick, how to throw a bucket over the side of a boat into the sea and how impossible it was to pick it up again full of sea-water – that sort of thing. A friend told him about the possible routes the skipper of a round-the-world yacht might take. These are the kinds of detail Michael cannot do without.

So far, so good. But his boy couldn't just *live* on the island. Something would have to go wrong – he'd need to run into some kind of trouble. As every

English teacher tells you, you have to have *conflict* to make a good story. Suppose the island wasn't uninhabited after all? Who – or what – might be on the island already? Michael remembered a newspaper story he had saved about a Japanese man who had lived for years alone on a Pacific island. During the Second World War, there was long and bitter fighting in the Pacific between the Japanese, who had occupied many of the islands, and the Americans. Eventually, the Americans drove most of the Japanese troops off the islands, and the remaining soldiers finally surrendered when the Americans dropped atomic bombs on the mainland Japanese cities of Hiroshima and Nagasaki. Here and there, however, a few Japanese soldiers had remained in hiding on the islands, not knowing that the war had ended, or scared of how the Americans might treat them. Most had eventually emerged from the jungle and made their way back to Japan. The newspaper story told of one soldier who had remained alone on an island, out of touch with the outside world, for 30 or 40 years. In the end, he had been found by chance and returned to his astonished family in Japan.

So, thought Michael, that might work. Suppose that the boy discovers he is sharing the island with a veteran Japanese soldier – or maybe a sailor. Two very different personalities with two very different purposes; the old Japanese warrior who wants to keep

his island the way he likes it – and the boy, young enough to be his grandson, desperate to get in touch with the outside world so that he could be reunited with his mother and father. Now *that* would be a conflict.

Time to start writing. Except Michael couldn't, because somehow, before he can start a story, he needs to know what his characters are *called*, and the names have to feel exactly right. And the names for these people just wouldn't come, any of them.

One day, still dreaming his story every now and again in his head, Michael found himself signing books in a school in London. A Japanese boy appeared at the head of the queue, and politely asked for Michael's signature in the book he had bought at the bookstall. 'Who shall I say it's for?' asked Michael, as he usually does. 'Kensuke' (he pronounced his name 'Kensky'). 'Brilliant,' said Michael, 'I'm just about to use your name in a story I'm writing. I'll send you a copy when it comes out!' (And he did.)

That was the old Japanese sailor sorted out, but there were several more names to go. Michael couldn't think what his stranded boy was called, and for want of a better name, he thought he'd call him 'Michael' for the time being, just to let him get started. That opened another door – if the boy was a Michael, it would feel wrong if he didn't tell the story in the first person. By the time Michael reached the end of the book, the Michael in the story had become 'Michael Morpurgo'. And in turn, that led Michael to write a postscript to the story which has brought him more letters from readers than anything else he has written.

Even naming the boat wasn't easy. Michael made a special trip to the marina at Torquay, but it was hopeless. The yachts all had names like *Sea Spray* or *Ocean Queen*. He wanted something *different*. Then, one day, sitting on his bed at home trying to write, the tune on the CD player downstairs nudged through his concentration. *If you knew/Peggy Sue/Then you'd know why I feel blue/That Peggy/ My Pe-eggy Sue-oo-oo/ Well, I lurve you gal/Yes, I lurve you Pe-eggy Sue!* A Buddy Holly number one from way back in the 1950s – one of Michael's boyhood favourites. He'd got it – the name was just right for the boat – no particular reason, and someone else might have preferred *Sea Spray*; but Michael knew he would enjoy sailing with his family on *Peggy Sue*.

Now surely he could start writing. Except there was that dog. He (or was it a she?) still hadn't got a name. One evening, Michael was walking down to Nethercott to see how the current group of City Children were enjoying life on the farm. He had his own dog, Bercelet (who crops up in *Arthur, High King of Britain*) with him. One of the boys from the visiting London school was hanging about in the lane.

'That your dog?'

'Yes.'

'Whad'ya call it?'

'Bercelet.'

The boy burst out laughing. 'Bercelet? What sort of name is that?'

Michael was offended on behalf of his dog. Bercelet was a noble name for a noble creature. Bercelet had feelings too. What's more, if you laugh at somebody's dog, you're laughing at *them*!

'Okay then, have *you* got a dog?'

'Yeah. Big one. Alsatian.'

'Well, what's yours called, then?'

'Stella Artois.'

Michael with his dog, Bercelet, 1998.

Michael tried to keep his face straight. 'Why d'you call her that, then?'

'Cos when we brought her home – when she was just a puppy – my dad was watching footie on TV. So we're going, "What shall we call her then?" Dad's drinking a can of lager and still trying to watch the footie. So he goes, "I don't care what you call 'er so long as you shut up and let me watch the football. Call her Stella Artois for all I care!" So we did.'

The cast was complete. *Kensuke's Kingdom* was up and running. Michael began at the beginning, as he always does – he doesn't write a bit here and a bit there, out of order, and then stitch them together. Before long, he had what has become his favourite opening to any of his stories:

.   I disappeared on the night before my twelfth birthday. July 28 1988. Only now can I at last tell the whole extraordinary story, the true story. Kensuke made me promise that I would say nothing, nothing at all, until at least ten years had passed. It was almost the last thing he said to me. I promised, and because of that I have had to live out a lie. I could let sleeping lies sleep on, but more than ten years have passed now. I have done school, done college, and had time to think. I owe it to my family and to my friends, all of whom I have deceived for so long, to tell the truth about my long disappearance, about how I lived to come back from the dead.

The Rainbow Bear (1999)

Michael watches a fair amount of television – and documentaries provide some of his favourite viewing. One evening, just before Christmas, he was absorbed in a programme about polar bears, enjoying the stunning sequences of the bears emerging from hibernation, sliding down snowy hillsides for the sheer joy of it, swimming with surprising speed and grace under water as they hunted for their food.

Then, in the middle of the programme, the telephone rang:

'Michael, it's Michael here. The other one.'

It was Michael Foreman again – the illustrator of so many of Michael's books. (*To avoid getting hopelessly confused, Michael Morpurgo appears as MM in the next few pages, and Michael Foreman as MF.*)

'Happy Christmas, Michael', said MM.

'Is it? Look, switch your TV on, there's something on you ought to watch.'

'I know. I'm trying to watch it – or I was, until you interrupted.'

After the programme was over, they spoke again. MM was excited by the idea of a polar bear story and MF was equally excited by the idea of polar bear illustrations.

Of course, MF can't begin work until MM comes up with a story. MM racked his brains and then racked them some more, but no story came. Not until one day when he was at home, sitting on his bed and thinking about doing some writing, and also looking out of the window, wishing it would stop raining so that he could go for a walk to clear his head. He didn't envy the sheep in the field over the hedge, hunched against the driving rain.

And then, suddenly, the rain stopped. The sun came bursting through and with the sunshine came a rainbow. In a moment, it seemed, a flock of rainbow-coloured sheep, now much more cheerful, was busily grazing.

If you could have rainbow sheep, why not a rainbow *bear*? MF would like that idea, MM thought – great for illustrations. With rainbows came the old notion of wishing upon a rainbow – you're supposed to get whatever you've wished for. The story was beginning to take shape – a bear like those playful, powerful bears in the TV documentary, a bear who somehow learns about rainbows and wishing on rainbows. How would he learn that, though? Perhaps, one day, the bear meets a wise old Inuit hunter, a shaman, who teaches him about wishing and rainbows. The bear then wishes himself into *becoming* a rainbow bear – and then what happens to him? Well, being a rainbow bear might bring its own problems – wishes don't always turn out quite as you expect …

*   *   *

The Rainbow Bear has other stories deep within it – tales told around the fire, long before stories were written down in books. In the very way the story is told, Michael echoes the rhythms of those tales. Such stories are often particularly good to read aloud, very like those Rudyard Kipling *Just So Stories* Michael loved as a small boy. *The Rainbow Bear* begins:

> I am snow bear. I am sea bear. I am white bear. I wander far and wide, king in my wild white wilderness.

Language was carefully crafted in the old tales. Sometimes a kind of rhythm comes through the use of alliteration, the repetition of particular letters at the start of words, as with all the 'w' sounds in that opening sentence. Michael had first met the use of alliteration when he read *Sir Gawain and the Green Knight* at university. Now he borrowed the idea to give both rhythm and a sense of strangeness to the picture book the two Michaels created together.

Here is the bear's description of his hunting:

> Seals are slow. Seals are best. I stalk them silently. Silently. I am snow bear in a world of white and they cannot see me coming. But one sound and a seal slips away into the sea.

Billy the Kid (2000)

'Hello, Michael. It's the other Michael again.'
This time, MF was inviting MM to go up to London to see a football match. Anyone who reads MF's picture book *Goal!* knows he's a Chelsea fan, and it was a Chelsea game he wanted MM to see. MM wasn't very interested. He much preferred watching rugby. In fact, he had never been to see a big football match and didn't particularly want to. On the other hand, invitations from MF often led to surprises or, at very least, an adventure. And more than once, they had led to stories. When MF said he was paying, MM said he'd go.

MM had to admit the atmosphere at Stamford Bridge, the Chelsea ground, was terrific. The place was packed out and once the game started, it took him quite a while to get the hang of how people behaved at football matches. In fact, he missed quite a few of the best moments since everyone around him stood up and blocked his view whenever something exciting happened. They didn't do that at Twickenham.

At half-time, MM asked MF why he'd wanted him to come all the way up to London from Devon to see a game.

'You see those six old blokes in red uniforms sitting in the Directors' Box up there?'

'Yes.'

'Well, they're all old soldiers – Chelsea Pensioners. They live at The Royal Hospital, just down the road. It's a kind of retirement home for ex-Army men. They get free seats in the Directors' Box for all the home games.'

'Excellent. I dare say Chelsea can spare a few free seats. So?'

'So now take a look down behind the goal at that end – the Shed End, they call it. Can you see just one bloke sitting there in one of those red uniforms?'

'Yes, I've got him.'

'Well, he could be sitting with the others in the Directors' Box, but he won't. You see, when Chelsea offered him a free seat there, he said, "Not likely. When I was little, my dad used to bring me to every home game, and we'd go behind the goal in the Shed and I'd sit on his shoulders so I could see properly. That's where I want my free seat, please – in the Shed right behind the goal." Michael, I want you to write that man's story. And I'm going to do the illustrations.'

So MM began to dream. There was a whole lifetime to be lived by that little boy perched on his dad's shoulders before he became the old soldier in his Chelsea Pensioner's coat at the Shed End. The two things Michael already knew about him were that he had always loved football and, given his age, he must have been a soldier during the Second World War.

Slowly, the story filled up. Michael drew on experiences of his two uncles – Peter and Francis. Then there was another story. A close friend of the Morpurgo family – a kind of 'unofficial uncle' to Michael – had served in the Royal Army Medical Corps in the Second World War. He had been one of the first Allied soldiers to go into the concentration camp at Bergen Belsen after the German guards had left in a hurry. He never fully recovered from what he saw on that terrible day. At the age of nineteen, he and his mates were ordered to help with the burial of 30,000 people. Then they'd had to try to nurse another 30,000 survivors back to health; most of them were in a terrible condition and despite the best efforts of the Army doctors, they never recovered. Many of the prisoners were just children, though they often looked like shrunken little old men and women. For many it was too late and the medical orderly and his friends could do little but watch them die. When he finally came home months later, he was haunted by those weeks at Bergen Belsen; what he had seen lurked in his memory for the rest of his life. The ghosts lodged in his dreams; it was very difficult for him to hold down a job and often he found escape from those ghosts only by drinking heavily.

*　*　*

Like that family friend, Michael's hero Billy is one of the first medical orderlies to reach Bergen Belsen. The German authorities built a wall of secrecy around the camps – civilians living within a mile or two of concentration camps had no knowledge of the brutal conditions and the daily slaughter in the gas chambers behind the barbed wire fences. Certainly, Billy and his mates had very little idea of what to expect:

As we drove in through the gates of Belsen in our convoy of ambulances, [the prisoners] came wandering towards us like ghosts, walking skeletons, some of them in striped pyjamas, some completely naked. They were staring at us as if we had come down from some other planet. The children would come up to us and touch us, just to make sure we were real, I think. You couldn't call them children – more like little old people, skin and bone, nothing more, hardly living. They all moved slowly, shuffling. A strange silence hung over the place, and a horrible stench.

It was our job to do what we could for the sick, to get them eating again. As for the dying, we were usually too late.

We buried the dead in their thousands, in mass graves. You didn't want to look, but you had to. Once you've seen such things you can never forget them. They give out no medals for burying the dead, but if they did I'd have a chestful. There was one little boy I found in his bunk. I thought he was asleep. He was curled up with his thumb in his mouth. He was dead. I wrote home, but I couldn't tell them what I'd seen. I just couldn't.

The Chelsea Pensioner's life story – his adventures in the war and the bleak time he had afterwards, including the heavy drinking – had come together pretty well. Except Michael couldn't find an ending. Finally, he discovered just what he was looking for, right down in the south of France, hundreds of miles from where he'd started out at Chelsea's ground at Stamford Bridge. But that's another story, and you'll find it when you reach pages 194–196 of this book.

Private Peaceful (2003)

Michael had never forgotten his chat in the late 1970s in the Duke of York at Iddesleigh with the old soldier whose memories had first set him on the trail of Joey's story in *War Horse*. A couple of other First World War veterans were regulars at the pub at about that time, and Michael was always hungry to hear of their experiences. One of them had grown up in Iddesleigh. In his boyhood, working on the land, he would have expected to lead a hard-working but peaceful life, much like his father and grandfather before him.

Now he was in the hell of the Flanders trenches, caught up in the chaos of war, never sure if today might be the day when he'd get a bullet with his name on it. One night he was ordered to go out on a patrol. Half a dozen soldiers, led by an officer, had to crawl across the area between the German and British front lines known as no man's land. When they reached the German trenches, they were supposed to capture a

German prisoner and bring him back alive to be interrogated. Headquarters said that they needed information about the strength and positions of the German troops and this was the only way to get it.

The men knew this was risky work. They stood every chance of being killed or taken prisoner. If they were very lucky, they would make it back to the British lines; if they were even luckier, they just might get back with their captured German. The only good thing was that when you were ordered to go out on patrol, you got an extra ration of rum, which was supposed to help you keep your courage up. If you were slightly drunk, the Army seemed to think you might not worry so much about getting shot.

On this particular night, the patrol reached the German trenches without anyone spotting them. No sentries seemed to be posted, so the British soldiers dropped quietly down into a trench. Suddenly they heard music playing on a gramophone. Then they saw a slit of light spilling from a dugout. Still no sentries. They crept closer. 'What do you want us to do, sir?' whispered the corporal. 'Pull the pins on your grenades and drop 'em through that slit', said the officer.

There was a huge explosion and, the old soldier told Michael, the next few moments burned themselves for ever on to his mind's eye.

Six or seven Germans lay dying or already dead in

what was left of the dugout. But one soldier was unharmed. It seemed he had just taken off his clothes, perhaps hoping to snatch an hour or two's sleep. Now he stood there, naked but splattered from head to foot with his friends' blood, staring in terror at the British soldiers. The old soldier told Michael, 'You see, that was when I knew for the first time that a German was just the same as me. Before, he'd been "Jerry" or "Fritz" – not really a person at all. Now he was just a man. Like I was.'

Michael too could never forget the picture the old soldier had conjured up. It haunted his memory for more than twenty years until it was ready to link up with several other strands of stories which Michael wove together to make *Private Peaceful*.

In the late 1990s, Michael and his friend Michael Foreman were both giving talks at a conference held in Ypres, site of a famous and terrible First World War battle. Ypres is now home to the In Flanders Fields Museum. The two Michaels went round the impressive exhibits together and afterwards they chatted about what they had seen with the curator, Piet Chielens. Michael (Morpurgo) had been powerfully struck by a photograph of a young soldier, shot for cowardice. Piet is an expert on cases of this kind. He invited his guests to look at the records of some of the military courts martial that had condemned such soldiers to death.

One soldier, aged 17, had fought all the way through the Battle of the Somme in terrifying conditions – more than 60,000 men were killed or wounded on the first day alone in that battle. After a long spell of duty, the young soldier had been sent back to a rest camp, a mile or two behind the front line. Even here, lying in his tent, the ceaseless thunder of the artillery echoed in his ears. Suddenly he turned to his friend and said quietly, 'I can't stand the noise of those guns any more. I'm going home.' He simply stood up, leaving his rifle and the rest of his kit behind him and walked out of the camp and away from the fighting.

He didn't run or make any attempt to hide – he just walked along the road. He'd gone no more than a couple of miles before the military police picked him up. Michael read aloud the transcript of the actual words spoken at the trial – it took no more than twenty minutes to read. Little more than the length of a morning break in school to decide whether a man should live or die. No help was given the boy to prepare his defence. In the courtroom, he had to speak for himself.

He was condemned to death and, six weeks later, he was executed at dawn. His friends from his own unit were ordered to make up the firing party which shot him, tied to a stake and blindfolded just a few metres in front of them. The commander of the

British Army, Field Marshal Haig, and his generals believed that if soldiers were required to execute one of their own mates, they would think twice before they deserted themselves. The men could not disobey orders – if they had done so, they too would have been shot. After the execution, the dead man's friends had to bury the body; but then they found a way to show those high-ranking officers how they felt. They kept watch in silent respect by the grave all through the day until night fell.

Michael has seen the official telegram that the Army sent to the dead soldier's mother. It simply gave his name, rank and military number and then: WE REGRET TO INFORM YOU THAT YOUR SON HAS BEEN SHOT FOR COWARDICE. That was all. Michael tried to imagine how the boy's mother would have felt when she opened that envelope.

At first, Michael could barely believe what he had discovered about the way the whole case had been dealt with; then, his amazement turned to anger. He *must* write this story. Later, walking among the neat rows of hundreds of gravestones in a military cemetery, he found a name for his hero: Private Peaceful.

There were many soldiers whose spirits were broken under the extreme pressures of fighting in the front line. Three hundred of them were shot for desertion or cowardice. In later wars, when soldiers have suffered such traumas, medical or psychiatric care has usually been provided. Even in the First World War, officers who broke down under the daily stress of life at the front were often sent back to the United Kingdom to recover in hospitals. Such concern was not commonly shown for ordinary soldiers.

Many years later, some countries recognised how unjustly these 'ordinary' soldiers had been treated. The New Zealand and French governments gave full pardons to all of their soldiers who had been convicted and executed in such circumstances. They recognised how important it was that the honour of these men should be restored, not least so that their families could feel that justice had been done to their memories. The British government acknowledged how terrible the experiences undergone by these young men had been; but, despite repeated efforts by lawyers acting for the men's families, the British authorities have consistently refused to give official pardons. It has even been suggested that the government does not wish to pay out heavy compensation to the families. Whatever the reasons, Michael thinks this stubbornness is immoral.

*   *   *

As he read the accounts of the trials, Michael saw that one soldier was described by a single word: 'worthless'.

The idea of calling any human being worthless lit a burning rage in Michael. When he was asked which book he had most enjoyed writing, Michael replied, 'I think *Private Peaceful* is the book I have enjoyed writing the most so far. I know it sounds bizarre, *enjoying* writing something like that, but I was so passionate about it that I lost myself completely in the book, and that's the best way to write.'

As you read *Private Peaceful*, the story of a young farm boy who one day could take the nightmare of the trenches no more and decided that he would 'go home', you may well sense Michael's intense anger driving his pen across the page.

From the Dream to
the Book

From the Dream
to the Book

There are as many ways of writing stories as there are writers of stories. Some authors like to be at their desks by 8.30 sharp, every morning, just as if they worked in an office or a bank. Michael has never been like that. His work at Nethercott, his visits to schools, his journeys around the United Kingdom and his trips abroad make regular 'office hours' impossible. He isn't that kind of person; he doesn't *want* to work at set times every day. Michael needs to live as well as write. Then he can draw on memories and conversations, places and people, as he dreams his stories.

Those dreams may be swirling around in his mind for weeks, months or even for a year before he is ready to write. Ted Hughes, whose book *Poetry in the Making* was so important to Michael as a young teacher, once gave Michael some advice which he has followed ever since. 'Never begin a story unless you are sure you can finish it. If you don't finish one story, it's harder to start the next.' He didn't mean that you have to know *exactly* how things will end – just that you need to have enough of a story in your mind to be certain that it will work out somehow. Sometimes Michael has to wait for just one more idea, experience or memory to fall into place before he can begin. And, following Ted Hughes' advice, he won't begin until he's sure there is a story waiting to be told.

But how does the dream turn into a book?

How does he decide who should tell the story? How far does he map out the plot before he begins to write? How does he work on the first sentences of a book? How does he describe the way characters look – or how they talk? How – and when – does he discover how a story should end? In the following pages, there are answers to those questions – and to several more – about the way Michael writes his stories.

Who Tells the Story?

Deciding who is going to tell the story is probably the most important decision of all. 'Where the book is being written *from* creates the story', says Michael. 'It's almost always the key.' Is it a character *inside* the story telling in the first person (I did this, I felt that) or is the story told from *outside* the plot in the third person (she did this, he felt that)? Where does Michael want his readers to be – inside the head of one of the characters, seeing everything from one point of view? If so, then he'll probably write in the first person. Or would the story work better if his readers have a more distant perspective, so that they could be taken swiftly from one place to another or even from one time to another? In that case, he will probably write in the third person. Then readers can be close to the thoughts and feelings of different characters at different times.

So settling on who is to be the teller opens a story up for Michael. In *War Horse*, for example, he could begin to write once he had decided that Joey, the 'war horse' of the title, would himself be the teller. Using an animal to tell a story was a daring step for Michael, especially when this was such a serious story about a cruel war. But Joey was the only one who saw the whole story – from the British, Belgian and German sides; so Joey had to be the storyteller.

In *Private Peaceful*, all the themes and characters in the book were coming together well, but Michael needed to decide who could tell the story of the young soldier condemned to death by firing squad. He wanted the story to be about the man – and also about the effect of his terrible experience upon his family. Who would know both the man and his family well enough?

One day, Michael was puzzling away at the problem of who should tell the story when, for no particular reason, his eye fell on an old wristwatch he had inherited. It stopped working one day and Michael took it in to the jeweller's. 'This is an interesting one', said the repairer. 'It's really old, you know.' He consulted a reference book. 'Yes, I thought so. Made in 1915.' Now, as he worried away at the problem of who should tell the story of Private Peaceful, Michael suddenly thought, '1915 … so this watch could easily have belonged to someone who fought in the First World War. What if that someone is staring at the watch the night before the execution, dreading the minutes ticking away to dawn?'

From that moment on, Michael knew how the book was going to end and he also knew who could tell the story. If you know the book already, you will surely feel that Michael's final choice of narrator helps to make *Private Peaceful* one of his best books – it's very difficult to put down, even though the reader also would like to stop the relentless ticking of that watch.

Mapping Out the Plot

Nowadays, much of Michael's planning happens in his head before he picks up his pen. When he first started to write he didn't trust himself to stay in control of a plot throughout the telling of a long story. He used to make a very careful chart, setting out headings and outlines for each chapter, with the ending fully worked out before he began to write. The trouble was that after he had used this strategy a few times, he began to feel that if *he* knew the ending before he started, then his readers would also be able to guess what was going to happen long before they got to the end of the book.

Now, with the experience of so many books behind him, he needs to know who will tell the story, a fair amount about his chief characters and a broad idea of what is likely to happen; but he doesn't want to know every detail. The plot needs some space to breathe, to allow the story the chance to lead him in some surprising directions.

Michael no longer makes a 1, 2, 3, 4, 5 sort of list of events. He enjoys the surprises and discoveries as he goes along: 'I tend to have a very good idea of where a story might go, but I leave room for the characters to determine exactly how it gets there.' Even though the characters are creations of Michael's mind, it often feels to him as if they have lives and opinions of their own. They insist on going their own ways, doing or saying something he had not originally intended. When they seem to say, 'We would never do *that*! We'd do *this*!' Michael knows that his characters and their story are really alive. That's exciting for him, and as long as he's excited, then he thinks his readers will be too.

First Pages

Michael works hard on the first few paragraphs of his stories – especially the first two or three sentences. Here are the opening lines of three of his books:

Before it happened, before the world went black about me, I used to read a lot.

(The Sleeping Sword)

Blodin the beast stalked the land. He drank only oil, he breathed only fire. When he roared, the earth shook and the people trembled. Town after town he razed to ruins, village after village.

(Blodin the Beast)

Of all the houses in all the streets, we have to move into Number 23, Victoria Gardens. Number 24 would have been fine; but no, we had to end up in Number 23, right next door to Number 22, and trouble, real trouble.

(Black Queen)

By the time they have read those first sentences, readers are almost certain to have questions they want answers to (Why's the world gone black? Who on earth is this Blodin who drinks oil and breathes fire? What's Number 22 got to do with whatever this trouble is, then?). Readers may also have an idea of what kind of story is on its way. Michael hopes they will already be 'hooked', keen to find out what happens next, feeling they *must* read on to find out.

Here now are the first couple of paragraphs from *Cool!*

I think a lot about Lucky, and I wish I didn't, because Lucky's dead. It makes me so sad. It was me that chose his name too. But Lucky turned out to be not so lucky after all. I want to cry, but I can't. What's worse is I don't know why I can't cry. I just can't.

Sometimes I tell myself that maybe I'm in the middle of a bad dream, a terrible nightmare, that soon I'll wake up and Lucky will be alive and everything will be just as it was. But dreams and nightmares only end when you wake up, and I can't wake up. I try. I try all the time, but I can't. So then I know it can't be a dream, that what happened to me and to Lucky was real and true, that Lucky is dead and I'm locked inside my head and can't get out.

In just those few lines, such questions as these might

already be running through a reader's mind: Who's Lucky? Who is 'I'? Why can't 'I' cry? Why can't 'I' wake up? How did Lucky die? And why is 'I' locked inside his or her head and can't get out?

The first few paragraphs, and especially the first sentences, can take Michael longer to write than several pages once the story is up and running. Sometimes, a first sentence just comes, but usually Michael will try several possibilities – he'll try this way of starting, then another way, and maybe then

another. Once he's sure he is on the right track, he'll polish and polish those early sentences until he's got them right.

He feels he used to take too long to get into the plot. Now he has learned to get into his story more quickly – partly through practice, but also through writing short stories, where a writer has to seize a reader's attention straight away. 'I like to make my openings as snappy as possible,' says Michael. 'Get straight in there.'

In one way or another, his opening paragraphs invite readers into the story. They might grab hold of readers; or, maybe, they ask more thoughtfully: 'Are you puzzled? Or curious? Do you like the kind of voice that's telling the story?' If the reader accepts the invitation, a good opening says, 'Then you'd better read on – and quickly!'

Getting the Words Down

Michael rarely works at a desk or a table. He usually sits upstairs on his bed with a pillow behind him and his knees up in front of him, just as his writer-hero, Robert Louis Stevenson, used to work. (Chairs and tables make Michael's back ache!) Here, he will do his thinking and, when the story's ready, he'll write. He even works on a story *in* bed, if you count waking up in the middle of the night with what might be a solution to some puzzle he was struggling with in the plot.

Once he gets going, Michael writes very quickly in longhand in primary school exercise books which he begs, borrows but never steals from schools on his visits. As he fills up little book after little book, he has a great feeling of getting somewhere – fast! Sometimes, he will break off to go for a walk around the lanes, to clear his head or re-think an idea, maybe dropping in at the Duke of York for some company and talk.

At this stage, he does not bother too much about his spelling, his punctuation or his paragraphs. He will take great care over all of these later, but for the moment, the important thing is to get the words down. If he stopped too often to make corrections, he would feel as though he had a kind of 'editor' sitting inside his brain, slowing him down, and whispering, 'Hold on a minute! You can't say *that*! Are you sure *that's* right? Better go back and check.'

For Michael, putting the brakes on his writing in that way would be boring and stifling. He would feel he was only half inside the story he is creating. He needs to be amused, frightened or excited by what he sees in his mind's eye, just as the characters he is writing about are amused, frightened or excited; then, he knows from experience, his readers will be amused, frightened or excited too.

He also listens with his mind's *ear*. He doesn't actually speak words out aloud as he writes, but he can hear the words in his head as they go down on paper, especially when characters are speaking. He thinks of what he does as *telling* rather than writing. He hopes each reader feels she or he is, individually, being told a story through the printed words.

At school, Michael was frightened by being asked to write – he hated feeling that he was going to be judged and that what he'd done would not be good enough. It took him years before he learned not to worry all the time about failing, about getting things wrong. It's fine, he now thinks, to make mistakes when he is writing his rapid first draft. That's how he finds out what he really wants to say and the best way of saying it. He can always tighten it up later. There will already be lots of crossings-out and scribbles in the margins, but these are changes in the plot, not in the grammar. He gives his little exercise books to Clare. She somehow unravels what he has written and word-processes a clear text for Michael – he avoids computers himself, ever since he lost a great chunk of a story and never found it again. Clare will usually add some suggestions too. Then Michael makes more changes and hands the pages back to Clare. A revised copy comes back to Michael, goes back to Clare, back to Michael, back to Clare – maybe six or seven times over.

Eventually, the manuscript is ready to go off to the publisher, who may make more suggestions for changes. A good publisher is invaluable, for Michael and even Clare can get so close to the story that they can no longer see what's working and what isn't. A publisher with no feel for a story can be a nuisance. When that is the case, there may have to be discussions and even arguments. Michael especially dislikes requests from publishers to spell out every last detail for children. His 40 years of experience of talking and listening to children have taught him that young readers are more intelligent than some publishers seem to think – children like to have some space in a story to use their brains. That's how the story comes alive in their heads. If you have been elected Children's Laureate and have written almost a hundred stories, you stand a good chance of having the last word in an argument.

After the careful process of revision, Michael is usually satisfied. Even so, he might return to one of his stories a couple of years later and see at once a better way of telling it.

How Characters Look

One of Michael's strengths is that he knows his weaknesses. He feels he does well when he is describing how characters feel and act, for example, but he thinks he is less good at describing how people *look*:

> My shortcomings include my physical descriptions of characters, and so when I can't do something, I do what a lot of writers do, I avoid doing it. I know a famous children's illustrator who can't do horses – if you looked in his books, you'd see his horses are always partly hidden behind bushes! I'm a bit like that.

He feels he will never be able to create the kind of characters that the fantasy writers J.R.R. Tolkien and Philip Pullman conjured up in Gollum in *The Hobbit* and the mighty armoured bear, Iorek Byrnison in *Northern Lights*. Michael has never written a fantasy story and does not expect he ever will. Instead, he usually bases his physical descriptions on people he knows, though he sometimes borrows from two or three real-life 'models' to make up a single character.

'I'm no good at imagining people out of nothing', says Michael, but it is possible that he is too critical of himself when it comes to his descriptions of how his characters look. Certainly, this is what James Walker thinks – James is the fine actor who played the Birdman in Theatre Alibi's stage version of *Why the Whales Came*, which made two national tours and also ran for a season in London's West End. When James is rehearsing a part, he makes a close study of every aspect of his character. When he was working on the Birdman, for example, James and his wife visited the Scillies to get a feel for the islands of Bryher and Samson. He tried also to listen to the accents of island people. But his main resource turned out to be Michael's original novel.

James needed to know how the Birdman looked, how he spoke, how he walked as well as what was going on in his mind. He makes detailed notes and draws all sorts of sketches and diagrams in his notebook as he prepares a part. Here are some of the extracts from *Why the Whales Came* that James jotted down:

He was like an owl, a flitting creature of the dark, the dawn and the dusk.

… even in the hottest summers he would always wear a black cape over his shoulders and a pointed black sou'wester on his head. From a distance you could hear him talking loudly to himself in a strange, unearthly monotone.

The Birdman went everywhere barefoot, even in winter, a stooped black figure that lurched as he walked, one step always shorter than the other.

The Birdman's distinctive footprints, the right foot broad and heavy, the left just half a footprint, five toes and the ball of the foot. It was always this left foot which dragged a continuous furrow through the sand from one print to the next.

The words he spoke were unformed and unfinished. They seemed yawned out rather than spoken and then thrown out from the top of his mouth.

'It was perfect', says James. 'He gave me everything.'

Very few directors are able to give actors such detailed advice – right down to which part of the mouth produces the voice! And the precise detail of the Birdman's movements led to James feeling 'You can't be called the Birdman without walking like a bird!'

Long after the first night, the Birdman grew and grew in performance. All the actors never lost their love for their characters and their story, even though they performed the play every day – sometimes twice a day – through three long runs.

So perhaps Michael is better at physical descriptions than he realises.

How Characters Think and Feel

Michael likes to start from something solid, so when he is building the personalities of his characters he begins with real people he knows. His friend Sean Rafferty, for example, was especially useful – he had so many rich and varied qualities. He appears, or *bits* of him appear, in characters such as the Birdman in *Why the Whales Came*, the Grandfather in *Toro! Toro!* and Grandpa in *Farm Boy*. The old gardener at Nethercott in *Sam's Duck* was based on Les Curtis, who worked at the farm after Sean's time there. Michael's children have appeared in different guises in several of his books. His oldest son, Sebastian, is very like the 'Michael' who tells the story in *Kensuke's Kingdom*, while the boy crouching in the early morning mist by the lake in *The Silver Swan* is his second son, Horatio; and there is something of his daughter, Rosalind, in Emilie in *War Horse*.

Unlike many writers for children, Michael makes

little use of *himself* when building personalities for his characters – apart from drawing on his boyhood experiences at prep school. Michael does not spend much of his time analysing himself or thinking about how other people see him. He is not, he says, particularly self-aware. 'I know what I feel and I know what I feel about the people around me, but I'm not very aware of the effect I have on those people. My children would probably agree with that.'

That lack of self-awareness is quite surprising in an author, but Michael is very honest about this. When he gives one of his many talks to audiences ranging from 30 children in a single class to several hundred adults at a conference, he knows he 'turns into someone else'. He becomes a performer and, when he's finished, he doesn't necessarily turn back into his more private self as soon as he has finished speaking. Since Clare doesn't particularly like being married to the performer Michael, she sometimes has to remind him to stop behaving as if he were still up there on the platform!

In his creation of characters, as in much of his writing, Michael sees himself as intuitive – he follows his instincts. He says he is like one of those painters who 'splashes paint at the canvas' when he brings characters to life on the page. If he's going to live for several months in the company of these people, he wants to know them pretty well before he starts writing; but he does not spend long hours making analytical notes about their psychological complexities. He doesn't want to pin them down like specimens to be studied in a scientific experiment – his writing would become too self-conscious and mechanical. The characters, and the whole story, would lack energy and spontaneity.

Once again, Michael has discovered what works best for him through practice, practice and then more practice. In this way, his confidence has grown, including his willingness to try new ways of writing. So, if you looked at two of his First World War novels, *War Horse* and *Private Peaceful*, side by side, you would probably decide that the characters in the second novel are more complex – and more interesting – than those in the first, written some twenty years earlier.

There is no doubt that Michael is still developing as an author; certainly, he is more excited than ever about writing his stories.

Places

Every time Michael goes to London's Waterloo Station to catch Eurostar to France – which he does four or five times a year – he is as excited as a small boy going on holiday. 'I *know* I'm going to Paris, and that I've been there dozens of times before. I *know* everyone will be shouting all the time and being very rude to each other – but it makes no difference. I still marvel like a child at cities, at landscapes or at the open sea.' He's just as excited when it's time for the annual visit to the Scillies.

His youthful excitement about the places he visits has led, he thinks, to one of the strongest features of his writing, his descriptions of the settings in which his stories happen. Places are particularly important to Michael because it was many years before he settled somewhere he felt he belonged. He has written very little about the areas in which he lived before Clare and Michael put down their roots in Devon: Hertfordshire, London, Essex, Kent, Hampshire, Sussex. As we saw in *The Butterfly Lion* and *The War of Jenkins' Ear*, he *has* written about his prep school, which felt, to the young Morpurgo, 'like a little island cut off from the rest of the world – it could have been anywhere'.

One of the pleasures of being a writer for Michael is the research he regularly makes into the places where he sets his stories. He needs to do this, he believes, if he is to convince himself – and his readers – about the truth of his story. He has to be sure that he has 'got it right'. Thus when the two Michaels (Morpurgo and Foreman) were planning their picture book about Joan of Arc, they went off to Orleans in central France together. They wanted to get a feel for the old city, and in particular to follow the route of Joan's triumphal entry into Orleans when she relieved the siege mounted by the English Army. They talked to people to find out what Joan still means to the citizens of Orleans. The curator of the local museum walked the streets with them, pointing out which buildings had changed since Joan's time and which had remained pretty much as they were then. The Michaels needed to know both old and new, for their modern day heroine, Eloise, retraces Joan's route when she also rides through the city surrounded by cheering crowds – this time in a pageant to celebrate the saint's life.

For Michael, the most satisfying feature of *Waiting for Anya* and *The Dancing Bear* is his creation of the atmosphere of the tiny mountain villages of Lescun and Borce in the High Pyrenees. The same need to know the place he is writing about lies behind his frequent use of his own village of Iddesleigh, with its village hall, the Duke of York pub and even some individual houses such as Burrow in *Farm Boy*. Then there are the Isles of Scilly, with their changing

May day at Iddesleigh.

weathers, magical shorelines and restless seas that always seem crowded with stories waiting to be told.

Michael knows he is good at seeing a place as it is now and yet also seeing how it must have been at an earlier time. So, when his friend Piet Chielens, the Curator of the In Flanders Fields Museum in Belgium, took him to visit what seemed to be a peaceful valley, Michael's knowledge, reading and storyteller's eye enabled him to see back through 80 years to the trenches of the German and Allied front lines. Here, in no man's land, the German soldier and the Welsh soldier, David, tossed a coin for Joey in *Farm Boy*. Piet also took him to the fields where some of the British soldiers had been shot for cowardice. It made Michael shiver to realise that the very ordinary hedge he was looking at was the actual place where these young men – boys, almost – had stood facing the firing squads.

When he was writing *The Amazing Story of Adolphus Tips*, Michael visited Slapton Ley in South Devon. He looked along the long stretch of road, shore and sea – a favourite spot now for holidaymakers. Here the American soldiers rehearsed for the invasion of the Normandy beaches on D-Day, 6 June 1944. In his imagination, he could see and even hear the different episodes of a story that for years was kept secret from the civilian populations of Britain and the United States. There had been the shelling by the Allied ships which destroyed the Slapton Ley Hotel and the homes of English villagers. The American landing craft had come sweeping onto the beach, the soldiers leaping into the surf. A mile or two out at sea, American convoy ships, loaded with men, had been surprised by a hunting pack of German E Boats armed with torpedoes; hundreds of men had been lost – more Americans than were killed on the first day of the invasion on D-Day itself. As Michael looked at the now tranquil landscape, the tragic series of accidents and mistakes came alive in his mind's eye. 'And that stays in my head – it's a solid thing.'

He was practising what he sometimes preaches to young writers: You have to drink it all in.

The Way People Speak

Storytellers working with a live audience have to be skilled at doing all sorts of voices. Jack has to sound a good deal more friendly than the Giant, and the Princess must not be confused with the Frog. Michael's early experiences telling stories in a classroom helped him from the start to develop a keen ear for the ways in which people speak. Now, he feels confident about his ability to 'hear' the different voices of characters talking in his head as he is writing. He thoroughly enjoys creating conversations, for dialogue is one of the sharpest ways of bringing his characters to individual life.

He tries to listen attentively to the way people speak around him every day and to use what he hears in his writing. He's lucky in that he regularly meets people of different ages from different parts of the country. The voices of some of the children in Michael's stories are borrowed directly from the young visitors from London, Bristol or Birmingham who come down to stay at Nethercott. Grandpa in *Farm Boy* writes his story about the First World War much as he might speak, which is in the rich Devonian manner of the older country people around Michael's home.

Michael has always enjoyed films; and some of his ability to write dialogue comes from his liking for movies. Working on scripts for adaptations of some of his own stories for film and television has taught him more about writing dialogue. Everything has to be communicated by the actions, facial expressions and words of the characters, without the help of a 'commentary' by a narrator. Each word has to count.

One of the most challenging voices Michael has ever conjured up was for Adie, a black soldier from Alabama in the Deep South of the United States, who appears in *The Amazing Story of Adolphus Tips*. The story is set during the Second World War, and Adie's way of speaking had to sound like a black American from the mid-20th century rather than one from the early 21st. Michael drew chiefly upon his reading and his knowledge of films of the period in creating Adie's voice. His way of talking would still show traces of the old 'slave talk' from the 19th century; he would, for example, use the term 'Missy' when talking to the young English girl who is at the centre of the story.

When he put similar words and rhythms into the

mouths of Little Luke and Bessie, characters recently freed from slavery in *Twist of Gold*, a newspaper critic attacked him ferociously for being condescending towards black people and putting 'incorrect' attitudes into the minds of young readers. Michael was both upset and irritated by this judgement. He thought it was the critic himself who was patronising young readers by suggesting that they would be incapable of understanding that characters belong to a time as well as to a place, and they should speak accordingly.

Sometimes, when creating a character from a distant period in history, Michael needs to adjust not only the words a character might speak, but the order of the words and hence the rhythms of the speech. In this example from *My Friend Walter*, the first speaker is the ghost of Sir Walter Raleigh from the end of the 16th century, the time of the first Queen Elizabeth. The reply comes from Elizabeth Throckmorton, a ten-year-old girl from our own time. The contrasts between the two speakers are even clearer when their words are read aloud:

'Blame not your brother, dear Bess, for he is much perplexed by what has passed. In truth I see in him something of myself as a boy – quick to temper and quick to tears, but he has a kind heart and will grow to a fine man.'

'He's a pig,' I said. 'Wasn't my fault his jug broke. It

was Humph [*the family dog*]. And he goes and tells everyone like that. Serves him right.'

Dialogue is probably the area Michael revises most when he is working on the drafts of his stories. Usually, the problem is that characters say far too much! They have to be firmly cut.

Keeping Up the Suspense

Michael knows his stories do not race along like the Alex Rider stories of Anthony Horowitz or the thrill-a-minute disasters which strike the Baudelaire children in Lemony Snicket's *A Series of Unfortunate Events*. In some of his earlier books, Michael thinks the pace was too leisurely. Now, through the experience of writing so many novels, he has developed a better ability to control the tension of his plot. He has also learned to vary the pace of telling, since even the most exciting adventures can become tedious if they are always told at headlong speed.

It's partly a matter of holding things back – of not quite telling readers everything they desperately want to know. Sometimes, he keeps readers involved by what he *doesn't* say rather than what he does say. And at other times, the interest is sustained by the tone of voice used for telling, enabling the reader to share the anxiety, the confusion or the excitement of the teller.

Michael feels most comfortable when he is telling the story from the viewpoint of someone who is actually *there*. Although this means that the plot can only go wherever the narrator goes, Michael thinks that this is his most effective method of getting his readers completely caught up in the story. He enjoys experimenting within that framework. For example, first person narrators tell the stories of *The Wreck of the Zanzibar*, *Out of the Ashes* and *The Amazing Story of Adolphus Tips* in the form of diaries, while the story of *Cool!* is running through the mind of ten-year-old Robbie Ainsley, lying in a coma in his hospital bed, unable to communicate with his anxious visitors (even though one of them is the great Gianfranco Zola, his favourite footballer from his favourite team, Chelsea).

The most important single element for Michael in maintaining the tension in a story is that he himself is excited by what is happening. This is even more true for him now than it used to be – perhaps because he has learned to trust that his own excitement will come through to readers in what he writes. Soon after his 60th birthday he was hunched up on his bed, struggling to find the right ending for a short story. Suddenly, he cracked it! Michael leapt off the bed, punching the air like a striker who has just scored the winning goal in the European Cup final, and yelling '*YES!*' As far as he knows, no one was within half a mile to hear the great Children's Laureate at work.

Endings

Endings can be tricky. Michael likes to save some kind of surprise for the reader, and that means leaving room for some kind of surprise for himself as the writer. Since he now deliberately avoids planning his endings in detail until he gets there himself, finding the ending to a story can be quite a tense experience. Sometimes, he has to wait and wait for an ending to emerge; he struggles to be patient, though he knows the wait is usually worthwhile. His best endings, he thinks, are those which are driven by the characters – the people in the story dictate the way things will turn out simply because they are who they are.

Quite often, when Michael is talking to children, someone will ask, 'Why are your endings so sad?' Letters from readers often ask the same question. The ending to *The Dancing Bear*, Michael thinks, provides an answer. He firmly believes it is one of his best, even though he knows quite a number of his readers think it is one of his worst. They think it is an unhappy ending, and it shouldn't be! Michael says, quite simply, that they are wrong. The story tells of Bruno, an orphaned European bear, discovered one day by seven-year-old Roxanne in the Pyrenean mountains. She is also an orphan, badly treated by her grandfather with whom she lives. Roxanne and Bruno grow up together, forging a powerful, loving bond. She has a great voice, and thanks to a lucky break, gets the chance to make her fortune as the latest French pop sensation. Roxanne (now about seventeen) chooses to abandon the village, and Bruno. The bear dies of a broken heart.

Readers have objected that Michael shouldn't have finished his story in this heartless way. Stories about girls and bears just shouldn't be like that! But Michael feels sure that Roxanne, at the age she was, *would* have chosen the bright lights and fame of the music industry – she might regret leaving Bruno, but she'd go all the same. He also knows that, like Bruno, animals die from broken hearts. One of the Nethercott donkeys died through eating poisonous ragwort from the hedgerow. His partner pined miserably and, one night, simply laid down and died too.

Michael argues that he has to go for the ending he knows is *right*, not the one that readers – or even his publishers – would like him to have. 'You have to keep to the integrity of the story', he says. Michael agrees with his character, the old lady who tells the story of the white lion in *The Butterfly Lion*, when she says to her young listener, 'You must remember … that true stories do not always end just as we would wish them to. Would you like to hear the truth of what happened, or shall I make something up for you just to keep you happy?'

Michael is especially fond of the endings to two of his best-known books. He thought he had finished *Kensuke's Kingdom* but then he realised he wanted something else – he didn't know what – so that readers would feel that they had been reading more than just a cracking adventure story. The answer came in the story's one-page postscript; a letter written by Kensuke's son to the 'Michael' who tells of his adventures in the story. Michael has had hundreds of letters about that postscript, asking for more details about what actually happened to him on the island. At least a third of them are from adult readers. Somehow the fact that the postscript was in the form of a letter – and the fact that the narrator is called 'Michael Morpurgo' – persuaded readers that *Kensuke's Kingdom* could not be an invented story. Michael enjoys that.

The ending to *Billy the Kid* did not arrive with anything like the same speed. Michael was pleased with the life he had woven for the Chelsea Pensioner whom Michael Foreman had pointed out on the terraces at the Shed End at Stamford Bridge. He knew what the very last pages in the story would be about, but something more needed to happen to Billy before he came to stay in the Royal Hospital, Chelsea.

Michael puzzled away at the problem, off and on, for months. Then, as quite often happens, the solution came when he wasn't looking for it. He was a long way from home, in Aix-en-Provence in the south of France. He was speaking at a festival and, one night, he was invited to supper with the organiser of the festival and her friends.

Over the meal, his hostess told him a story. 'I live with two men', she said. Michael raised a polite English eyebrow. 'You see', she said, 'I live with my husband and with Henri. He's an old tramp who moved into our house for a night to keep out of the rain while it was still being built.' Five years later, Henri was still there, more or less part of the family. One difficulty did crop up – Henri used to get drunk rather frequently, just as Billy in Michael's story had problems with his drinking after his grim wartime experiences at Bergen Belsen. There'd been one or two crises with Henri, but in the end, after some tough talking and hard bargaining, a deal had been struck. Thus far things were working out pretty well, said Michael's hostess, with Henri living in a comfortable wooden hut at the bottom of the garden.

Michael went on listening and asking questions, discovering more details of the story, seeing already that the build-up to the ending he'd been searching for to complete *Billy the Kid* was becoming clearer, moment by moment, almost like a print in a photographer's developing dish.

Working with Illustrators

When you pick up a book with 'Words by So-and-So' and 'Illustrations by Someone Else' on the title page, you might well think that So-and-So and Someone Else must have spent hours and hours planning the book together. Surely, they would need to talk about which bits of the story could best be described by the words, which bits by the pictures, which by both, and so on.

In most cases, such meetings do not take place. Often, the publishers do not arrange for the writer and the illustrator to meet, but Michael refuses to work in this way. The risk would be that the illustrator might miss the 'flavour' of the story altogether. Therefore he insists on working closely with artists, especially with his favourite illustrators, Christian Birmingham, Quentin Blake and Michael Foreman.

Michael Foreman (MF) is the illustrator with whom Michael Morpurgo (MM) has collaborated most closely. MM sometimes says that he is not a 'natural writer' – the very first idea for a story quite often starts with an invitation or suggestion from someone else. Several of the picture books he has produced with illustrations by MF began with suggestions from one Michael to the other Michael – in some cases, neither can remember which Michael came up with the original idea.

MF is just as keen on getting things right as MM. When they were working together on *Joan of Arc*, for example, MM received a telephone call from MF, asking him what was the difference between French soldiers' helmets and English soldiers' helmets in the 15th century. Even though MF probably guessed MM wouldn't know the answer (and MM didn't know about the helmets, though the British Museum did), the two still chatted over the problem. MF usually invites MM to visit his studio to see how the paintings or drawings for a story are coming along. That's what working together is about for them – sharing everything from first ideas to final details.

After a while, when authors know their illustrators, they write episodes which they think their partners would enjoy painting or drawing. Good illustrations do not merely decorate a story. In books like *The Rainbow Bear* and *Dolphin Boy*, the story is made by

Michael with Michael Foreman after winning
the Favourite Children's Book Award, 2000.

the words and pictures working together to tell the
story.

What Michael Morpurgo enjoys about working
with the other Michael is that the two of them are
playing a kind of game. One Michael sets the other
challenges, almost daring him to take some risks,
asking him to go just a little beyond what he knows he
can already do. That's the fun of it, the joy of creating
a story together, to produce a book which neither
could have managed on his own.

A Tale of Two Laureates

A Tale of Two Laureates

Michael had finished the milking on the farm one evening in the late 1970s and thought he'd walk home along the path by the river. Sometimes it helped to take a bit longer to move from one world to another – from Nethercott and its excited visitors to home and the family.

Suddenly, in the dusk, a tall, dark figure in long waders climbed up out of the river. He stood waiting in Michael's path, fishing rod in hand: a handsome man, but rather grim, a little threatening even.

'You're the chap who's running this scheme up at the farm for kids from the cities, aren't you?'

Maybe it was the Yorkshire accent, or maybe it was a memory of a photograph he'd seen somewhere, but Michael suddenly realised who it was: Ted Hughes, the famous poet whose book *Poetry in the Making* had been such an inspiration to Michael as a young teacher ten or more years ago. Michael remembered he'd heard Ted lived not too far away and he also knew he was a keen angler. He'd even written poems about fishing.

So began one of the most important friendships of Michael's life. Since his boyhood days in Yorkshire, Ted Hughes had loved the countryside. Many of his poems are based on the close observation of animals. He became very interested in Farms for City Children, since the project worked out in practice what Ted deeply believed; that children needed to be in touch with the countryside, to know how it worked, to enjoy the contact with animals, with nature itself. As *Poetry in the Making* had shown, when children have the kind of experiences they were having every day at Nethercott, they found they wanted to write – often quite brilliantly – about what they were seeing around them. Ted was a great supporter of the scheme for the rest of his life and was delighted to be the first president of Farms for City Children.

Michael and Clare became close friends of Ted and his wife Carol. You have to like and trust another writer before you share your work, but before long Michael and Ted were regularly swapping whatever they were working on at the time. Ted would ask Michael what he thought of a poem or a story and, though he was – and still is – a little in awe of the Great Man, Michael would show Ted his work in return.

In 1982, Michael's book *War Horse* was in the running for the Whitbread Prize for Children's

Michael and Clare on holiday with
Ted and Carol Hughes, 1983.

Literature. This was the first time Michael had had a
book on the shortlist; he couldn't help but be excited.
He had written only a handful of books by then, and
this was his first major full-length novel. He knew
success in the Whitbread would not only help sales of
War Horse – he would also become a writer whose
stories publishers would be eager to accept.

The announcement of the winner was shown live
on national television and Michael thought he stood a
good chance of winning. He didn't, and what made
things worse was the brief comment made to him
by the Chair of the judging panel, Roald Dahl. 'Nice
book, yours. But, you know, children don't like
History.' Michael remembered he was on television

205

and just about managed to stop himself kicking the shins of the distinguished Chair of the judging panel. He *knew* that, for once, the author of *Charlie and the Chocolate Factory* and all those other best-sellers was simply wrong. Time after time, with stories like *Farm Boy*, *Twist of Gold* and *The Wreck of the Zanzibar*, he's proved that many children are fascinated by the adventures of people in other times. It all depends how the story is told.

Back at Iddesleigh, a day or two after the judging, Michael was still feeling sorry for himself when a car crunched to a stop on the gravel outside. It was Ted Hughes. 'Right, come on, Michael. Let's go out for the day.' Ted took Michael off to Bideford on the North Devon coast. They toured round a few bookshops, saw a couple of friends and had a pub lunch together.

Ted was a good Yorkshireman and good Yorkshiremen don't waste words in idle chat. After a while, though, Ted said something to Michael which he's never forgotten and which has helped to shape the rest of his writing life:

> *War Horse*, Michael. I've read it. It's a good book. In fact, it's a very good book. But you're going to do better.

That was exactly what Michael needed to hear just after he'd missed winning the Whitbread. It's what any hard-working writer needs to hear, whether they are 9 or 90 years old. Michael doesn't think he would have given up writing – storytelling is in his blood – but Ted's words gave him a new sense of confidence. If Ted Hughes felt Michael could do better, then Michael could. And would. Without those words, he might have stuck safely to what he knew he could already do pretty well; he would not have developed that love of adventure and experiment as a writer which is what drives him on. To this day, he hears Ted telling him, 'But you're going to do better.'

Michael thinks he has indeed done better, but despite all the stories Michael has written and the prizes he has won since that conversation, *War Horse* is still Clare's favourite book. When he's giving talks, Michael sometimes mentions this and asks in mock despair, 'Why would you stay married to someone like that!?'

One evening ten or more years later, Michael and Ted were relaxing by the fireside after sharing a feast of salmon. Ted was by now the Poet Laureate, a post which gave him the opportunity to bring poetry more into the public eye, for his opinions were frequently requested by the media. And when they weren't requested, he often made his views known anyway.

This is how Michael describes what happened in the next few very important minutes. Michael is 'the storyteller' and Ted is 'the great poet' in Michael's account:

The storyteller asked the great poet whether he considered his stories and poems for children to be lesser in any way than his stories and poems for adults. 'Not at all,' he said.

'So why, in that case', asked the storyteller, who wrote books mostly for children, 'why is it that children's literature, however good, is generally considered to be inferior, of less significance than adult literature?'

'Probably because children are thought to be less significant', said the poet. 'A good book', said the great poet, 'a well written book, is significant, whoever it is for.'

The storyteller looked into the flames and had a sudden, exciting idea, the kind he sometimes has when a new story first comes into his head. He spoke his idea. 'What if there were to be a Children's Laureate?' he said. 'Not a regal role, like yours is, but someone who would enthuse children and adults alike, with children's stories and poems and illustration and drama – do you think it might make a difference as to how the world perceives children's literature?'

'A terrific idea', said the great poet, which both pleased and surprised the storyteller. 'So why don't we do it?' the poet went on – which was not at all what the storyteller had in mind. It had just been an idea to him. 'I know just the person who could bring the whole thing together and make it happen – Lois Beeson', said the great poet. 'You know her, you ask her.'

That's how the idea of a Children's Laureate started. The more they talked about it, the better the idea seemed. After all, the United Kingdom was the country of all kinds of great children's writers – Lewis Carroll, Rudyard Kipling, A.A. Milne, Robert Louis Stevenson, Edith Nesbit, Arthur Ransome – and there were illustrators like Kate Greenaway, Randolph Caldecott and Edward Ardizzone and E.H. Shepard who drew the pictures for *Winnie-the-Pooh*. What about all the more recent writers like Joan Aiken and Mary Norton and Alan Garner – and illustrators like Quentin Blake and Anthony Browne and dozens of others? Other countries envied Britain for its children's books, and yet the British themselves seemed to make very little of it. It didn't make sense.

Ted was right about Lois Beeson – she really was just the person to bring everything together. She seemed to know everyone who worked in the children's books field. Lois and Michael talked to other people and other people talked to other people, and after much work, the position of Children's Laureate was established.

To Michael's great sadness, Ted Hughes did not live to see the dream by the fireside come true; he died in 1998. The first Laureate was appointed the following year – the magical Quentin Blake, whose illustrations for the books of Roald Dahl and Michael Rosen, as well as his own picture books like *Mr*

Magnolia or *Mrs Armstrong on Wheels*, are loved by children and adults alike. Quentin Blake began the work which he has continued long after his two-year term as Laureate, helping the nation to become more aware of illustrators for whom Britain has been internationally famous in the last quarter of the 20th century – artists like John Burningham, Shirley Hughes, Anthony Browne, Jan Ormerod, Raymond Briggs and Michael Foreman as well as Quentin Blake himself.

In 2001, the novelist Anne Fine took over as Laureate. She continued to make the general public much more aware of stories and poems for children. One of Anne Fine's themes was to challenge some aspects of the literacy programme in the National Curriculum, which shapes what children are taught in schools – a concern shared by Michael and many other leading writers. They feel passionately that children are not given enough time to experience the sheer fun and joy of reading and that they have too few chances to express what is important to them in their writing. If they miss out on such things, then why would children actually *want* to read and write better? Anne is a witty and forceful speaker and, says Michael, 'She shook things up and rattled a good number of cages which needed rattling. Everywhere she went, she created strong debate about ideas and raised the prestige of children's literature.' Anne

Fine is really good at starting useful arguments – and she's pretty good at finishing them, too!

When Michael was asked if he would be willing to be nominated as the Children's Laureate to follow Anne Fine, he wasn't at all sure whether he should stand for election. For one thing, he thought there were probably stronger candidates around. Although the time had come for Clare and Michael to retire from their full-time work at Nethercott, he wasn't sure he could fit in all the necessary travel and talks alongside his writing. But, the Laureateship had been his idea in the first place, and he knew he would like to do the job sometime. If he couldn't cope with the work now, he surely couldn't when he was older and, maybe, less energetic.

When he was appointed to the Children's Laureateship in May 2003, Michael seized the opportunities the position offered. His beliefs and his message were straightforward. He wanted children to get back to the joy of reading and listening to stories. He accepted that a new emphasis on literacy in schools had been necessary in the 1990s – there had certainly been room for improvement in the ways reading and writing were sometimes taught. He does not think that the Literacy Hour is a waste of time, though he does wish it were called the 'Literature Hour' and he is not happy with the way some of the hour is used. He thinks that the emphasis on grammatical detail and the pressures of testing and record-keeping heaped upon children, teachers and schools by the government, have gone far too far.

Stories, he decided, would be the heart of what he would talk about as he went around the nation:

> The reason that stories were written was not to test children in English lessons. Stories were not written so that questions could be asked about them. First and foremost, children should love the literature, whether it is stories, poetry or plays. I want children, parents, teachers and librarians to create and enjoy that love together – *then* children will happily go on to learn about why a character does such-and-such – they'll go on because they love the book so much and they'll have all kinds of ideas about it already. Then they'll really *want* to know more. I want them to have the time and chance to read *all* of a story, not just a couple of chapters here, or a paragraph or two there, with no time to read the rest before they have to answer questions about what they have read.

So Michael set off on a series of long tours around the British Isles. He visited far corners of Scotland, England, Wales and Northern Ireland, he went to small schools, villages and towns which did not usually have visits from writers. He spoke frequently at festivals, teachers' meetings and conferences. He became involved in BookAid International, which sends books to countries where people are hungry for books as well as food. He made plans to go himself to such countries. He wanted to see children in the United Kingdom making a decision, with the help of BookAid, to send a copy of their favourite book to a child overseas starved of books.

He also found that others shared his vision of bringing literature to wider audiences. He discovered people who, like himself, were willing to think big. If young people flocked to rock concerts, maybe they would also flock to story concerts. In Wales, Michael met Ruth Hay, who was already organising a series of

Michael and Clare in Russia with Kevin and Linda Crossley-Holland, Cherie Blair and the wife of the Russian President, Mrs Putin.

story concerts there for audiences of ten, eleven and twelve-year-olds. Ruth and Michael called a group of influential people together to plan exciting concerts for audiences of up to a thousand in great cities like Glasgow, Belfast, Oxford and Cardiff, finishing up at the Albert Hall in London. Stars of the children's literature galaxy like Benjamin Zephaniah, Jacqueline Wilson, Eoin Colfer, Malorie Blackman and Louis Sachar were all willing to give their time to read and tell their stories and poems at the concerts. As Children's Laureate, Michael would attend all the events, performing himself and also introducing the other novelists, storytellers and poets.

All of this work took a huge amount of time and effort. The organisers spent many hours making phone calls, writing letters, sending e-mails and faxes, booking the halls and speakers, making all the detailed arrangements for the concerts and, very importantly, securing sponsorship.

Despite all this complex administration, Michael's message at the heart of everything is simple, whether he is speaking or telling stories in the Albert Hall or in a small village primary school hundreds of miles from London. It is his belief in the need of children, and of adults, to hear and enjoy stories, and in the way in which stories help to shape the way we live our lives.

The Morpurgo File

The Morpurgo File

The entries in 'The Morpurgo File' reflect the wide range of interests in Michael's life, from what he reads in his spare time to what kind of music he likes. There are entries about what he thinks about prizes and film, television and stage versions of his stories. There are sections about his beliefs – and also about what he thinks he might write in the future. For him, there is always something more to be attempted, something just over the horizon, so that he feels he has to keep striding on, eager to find out what's waiting for him, just out of sight.

Michael and His Reading

Michael does not read many novels and short stories by other authors. He admits that there are two basic reasons for this neglect, 'both of them stupid'.

First, he feels hugely envious if someone else discovers a subject he wishes he had thought of first – and that prevents him from enjoying the book because his irritation keeps getting in the way. Secondly, he has spent such a large part of his life learning and practising the craft of writing that he is sometimes impatient with others' work, especially if he feels the writing is 'lazy' or careless. He feels ashamed of both these reactions, but he is honest enough to admit that he can't help himself. That's how it is.

The rhythm of Michael's life probably doesn't suit reading novels – ideally, you need good long stretches of time. At home, there has been the running of the farm, spending time with the visiting children, replying to letters, answering telephone calls and e-mails –

and he enjoys time with friends and family. Then there are his visits to publishers and his agent in London, his speaking engagements at festivals, schools and libraries around Britain, his trips to France, his tours as far afield as Russia, Australia, Canada or Uganda. (He's not much good at saying 'No' to invitations.) When he is travelling on a train or a plane, he might well be dreaming a story or, if he is reading, he will probably be delving into some non-fiction as he researches information for his latest book. And on top of all that, there's his writing.

For his own enjoyment, he usually reads poetry. He has published a few poems himself but he doesn't – yet – think of himself as a poet. He still has much to

Michael reading to children in the barn at Nethercott.

admire and learn with none of the irritable reactions which can get in the way of his reading of novels and short stories. He reads widely and frequently in poetry – you can read, and re-read, many complete poems in quite a short space of time; there is usually a book of poems by his bedside or even in the bathroom.

He sometimes returns to two of the childhood favourites he first met when his mother and his grandparents read to him – Robert Louis Stevenson and Rudyard Kipling. He reads poems by Ted Hughes often. Although Ted died in 1998, the inspiration of his friendship is very much alive, and his poems still draw the two men close together.

Michael shared with Ted Hughes an admiration for the poems of Charles Causley. After spending the Second World War in the Royal Navy, Causley returned to the town where he was born, Launceston, in Cornwall. There, he taught for most of his working life in the local primary school. Maybe for him, his daily work with children fed his poems just as the visitors to Nethercott have sustained Michael's writing. Michael loves the way Causley can tell a subtle or mysterious tale in verse – he makes it all seem so simple. 'But you just try to do what he does yourself', says Michael. 'It's incredibly hard work to make everything seem so effortless.' Michael has compiled several collections of poetry – his problem was to limit the number of Causley poems he had room to include.

Michael and Music

Michael has won many prizes and received several honours; but he really felt he had finally 'made it' when he was invited to be Sue Lawley's guest on *Desert Island Discs*, the longest-running programme on BBC radio. The basic idea is that a famous person is supposed to be stranded on a desert island with eight pieces of music of their choice and the equipment to play them. Sue Lawley chats with her guests about their lives and also asks them to talk about the reasons for their selections. Michael decided he would take this seriously; after all, 'Michael Morpurgo' had got on pretty well in *Kensuke's Kingdom*, so he ought to know a thing or two about surviving on desert islands. His choice would reflect the story of his life and also help him to keep his spirits up when he was on his own, which Michael doesn't really enjoy for long periods.

Michael and Clare's home is often filled with music as they go about their work; and much of that music

Michael has loved all his life. 'Seventy-eight' records used to spin on the turntable much of the day in his childhood homes; and music, along with sport, was his salvation at school. That music was often classical – Mozart is a particular favourite for both Clare and Michael. But he had also been a boy when Elvis was King and Teddy Boys were ripping out the seats of cinemas and dancing in the aisles to the beat of Bill Haley and the Comets in 'Rock Around the Clock'. There were not too many Teddy Boys at King's School, Canterbury, but few teenagers in the 50s were not caught up in the excitement of rock 'n' roll.

These were the eight records that Michael selected to take with him to keep him sane and cheerful on his desert island:

1. Mozart: *Exultate Jubilate*.
   To remind him of his mother and his grandparents and the music that surrounded him in his boyhood. The religious nature of the piece would also remind him of all those hours singing in the quiet beauty of Canterbury Cathedral.
2. Mozart: *Clarinet Concerto*.
   Because it is Clare's favourite. He didn't think he was likely to forget her, but just in case ...
3. Buddy Holly: *Words of Love*.
   Elvis was massive, but Buddy Holly was right up there too when Michael was in his teens. Buddy Holly's tragic

death in a plane crash cut off a career that was probably not yet at its peak. This one, Michael thinks, is his best.

4. The Beatles: *Here Comes the Sun.*

   If you were young in the 60s, how could you not take a Beatles record? This one is very optimistic and Michael thought he might need cheering up when he woke to another day alone on the island.

5. Thomas Tallis: *Spem in Alium.*

   A very special choice to remind Michael of one of the most moving moments of his life. The piece was sung by the 40 voices of the Tallis Singers (there is no musical accompaniment) at Ted Hughes' funeral in Westminster Abbey. As the echoes of the voices faded away, there was utter silence, broken eventually by the recorded voice of Ted Hughes himself reading, from Shakespeare's play Cymbeline, *a poem about death which begins:*

   > *Fear no more the heat o' the sun,*
   > *Nor the furious winter's rages;*
   > *Thou thy worldly task hast done …*

6. A dance tune from the film of Brian Friel's play, *Dancing at Lughnasa.*

   A moment that Michael loved in the theatre and on film. Despite the harshness of their lives, all the characters on stage are drawn one by one into a joyful dance to the rhythm of an infectious Irish tune, playing on the radio. Michael rather fancied leaping about to this tune on the beach of his island. After all, he'd be on his own.

7. Coope, Boyes and Simpson: 'The Burning Mill at

Messines', from a CD entitled *We're here because we're here*, which includes old songs from the First World War and a number of new songs written by the group about that war.

When the ideas that gave birth to Private Peaceful *were first stirring in Michael's mind, he visited a conference at Ypres. The folk trio, Coope, Boyes and Simpson performed there and it was then that he heard this tune played on the pipes.*

8. Beethoven: *The Pastoral Symphony.*

On the cover of a book Michael owned as a boy, Beethoven strides across a hillside, hands behind his back, hair flying in the wind, tailcoat streaming out behind him. The symphony moves from a peaceful day to a storm and then back to tranquillity again – just like the Devon weather, which Michael knows very well as he too strides about the hillsides, with a crowd from Farms for City Children trailing behind him.

The castaway on *Desert Island Discs* is allowed to take one book and one 'luxury' to the island. Michael cheated a bit with his book by choosing an anthology of over 450 poems, *The Rattle Bag*, selected by Ted Hughes and another friend, Seamus Heaney. You can read poems over and over again and still get something new from them, he thought – in fact, he might even try to learn some of them by heart. For his luxury, Michael tried asking for a radio, but was told very firmly by the lady from the BBC that he was being ridiculous. So he asked his granddaughter what he should take. Her answer made him giggle. 'What you'll need after you've been skipping about on the sand, Grandpa', she said, 'is a water slide.'

So that's what Michael took.

Michael and Film,
Television and Theatre

When the thirteen-year-old Michael was so deeply impressed by the rhythms of Paul Schofield's voice as he played Hamlet in the late 1950s, he could hardly have dreamed that, some 30 years later, the great actor would be playing in the film of one of his stories. Yet it was indeed Paul Schofield who played the Birdman in a film of Michael's book, *Why the Whales Came*. Schofield was not the only famous actor involved – the cast included Helen Mirren and David Suchet, both known to millions of television viewers all over the world as very different detectives in the *Prime Suspect* and *Poirot* series.

Michael wrote the film script for that movie, which was shot on Bryher in the Isles of Scilly, where the original novel was set. The whole project almost collapsed halfway through. All the crew were on Bryher at one point, taking up the accommodation usually used by summer visitors. Then the money ran out. The film people said they were leaving. The islanders said, 'No, you're not. You've booked for the summer and we won't let you off the island.' That little difficulty took a while to sort out before the film could be completed. Michael has a souvenir of the film hanging on his sitting-room wall – the three-metre long artificial narwhal horn used in the movie.

Friend or Foe, *My Friend Walter* and *Out of the Ashes* have also been made into films for television or the cinema. Several more stories are under consideration. Michael finds the writing of film scripts a demanding skill that he is still learning, teaching him useful lessons in the writing of dialogue in the process. He thinks *My Friend Walter* and *Out of the Ashes*, the novel about the Foot-and-Mouth outbreak in Devon in 2001, are in some ways better as films than they were as novels. However, the difficulty with films, especially for television, is that they have to be squeezed into a particular time slot. *Out of the Ashes* had to be told in just half an hour – which made it difficult for the viewer to have a sense of the long, drawn-out nature of the disease that, in life as in Michael's story, drove farmers into terrible bouts of depression.

The theatre can offer more freedom and excitement than cinema or television, in Michael's experience. *The Butterfly Lion*, *Kensuke's Kingdom*, *Why the Whales Came* and *Private Peaceful* have all been adapted for the stage. What has fascinated Michael is

what happens to his novels when they are trans-
formed into around two hours of live action. With the
involvement of actors, a director, lighting and sound
designers and stage crews, the story becomes 'ours'
rather than simply 'his'. Even the audience has a
share in bringing the play to life for each particular
performance.

The rehearsal process often seems to him
mysterious and chaotic when he drops in to watch a
production in its early stages. Yet when he attends the
performance, he is delighted by the imagination that
can bring to life a boat adrift in dense fog in *Why the
Whales Came* or the complex tale of *Private Peaceful*,
told by just a single actor. Then there were the deaths
of hundreds of Japanese people when the atomic
bomb dropped on Hiroshima in *Kensuke's Kingdom*.
That particular effect was created in the Polka
Theatre production in Wimbledon through the use of
puppets, a sudden surge of blinding white light and
then, as the dazzled audience's vision refocused, a
mound of charred corpses – different puppets – on the
stage. Michael was stunned – it was his story and a new
story at the same time. The Japanese ambassador,
who had also been in the audience, stood up after the
show to make an unscheduled speech, saying how he
felt the play could help in developing understanding
between nations and how much he hoped children in
Japan would also have the chance to see the production.

Michael and Prizes

Michael feels pulled in opposite directions about prizes and awards for children's authors and illustrators. There are quite a number of them now, whereas 40 years ago there was only the Carnegie Medal (first awarded to Arthur Ransome's *Pigeon Post* for the best book of 1936). The medal is simply that, with no financial reward for the author. Now prizes can bring a writer as much as £10,000, as well as a large increase in sales of books.

Michael is glad that children's books now attract more attention through these awards, which are widely reported in the media. That's good for trade for all children's writers and illustrators. The problem with prizes is that if you are shortlisted – in the last four or five – then you would not be human if you didn't want to win. That's where the difficulties start, says Michael.

If you win, then you feel a kind of triumph which is more like winning a boxing championship or a tennis final at Wimbledon than anything to do with writing a book. That kind of competition with other writers isn't good for you, especially when everyone is really on the same side – you all want more children to read more books. If you lose, you feel miserable and start to invent excuses to explain why you didn't win. ('Just look at those judges – what do *they* know about real children?')

Being human, Michael wished he had won the Whitbread Prize in 2004 for *Private Peaceful*, even though he much admired the winner, David Almond's *The Fire-Eaters*. He did win the Whitbread in 1995 with *The Wreck of the Zanzibar*, the Smarties Prize (chosen by children themselves) in 1996 for *The Butterfly Lion*, and the Children's Book Award for *Kensuke's Kingdom* in 2000 and for *Private Peaceful* in 2004 (selected by panels of children from all over the United Kingdom). Michael has had some twenty books translated into French. He has won the Cercle D'Or Prix Sorciere in France on three occasions. He was especially pleased by the award in February 2004 of the title 'Chevalier de L'Ordre des Arts et des Lettres' by the Ministry of Culture and Communication.

In July 2004, he was honoured by his 'local' university at Exeter when he was given an honorary doctorate, which has nothing to do with medicine but which does mean Michael could now call himself Doctor Morpurgo, if he chose to. (Universities award the title of 'Doctor' to distinguished people for all kinds of academic subjects.) The small boy struggling, and often failing, to grind out essays that would satisfy his prep school teachers would have been amazed to know that, half a century later, he would receive such a high honour from a university in recognition of his writing.

In the end, though, Michael's continuing ambitions are nothing to do with awards or honours, agreeable though it is to have his work recognised. He is much more interested in the story he is writing at the moment.

Michael, Reviewing and 'What Really Matters'

Michael doesn't read all the reviews of his books which appear in newspapers and magazines. He found he used to ignore the praise and remember only the occasional word of negative comment. Usually, his reviews are favourable, but every now and again reviewers seem to want to draw attention to themselves rather than the books they are supposed to be writing about. He thought it foolish, for example, when a reviewer said that the Devon farm boys who had to go to war in *Private Peaceful* could not possibly have thought and spoken in the way that Michael had described. What did a London-based reviewer know about how Devon farm boys thought and spoke? Michael knew these men personally – they were his friends.

Michael also feels irritated when reviewers, or people asking questions at conferences, suggest that he preaches to children; as if, through his stories, he is trying to tell children what they ought to think. It is true that Michael believes strongly in values which may sound old-fashioned. He admires, for example, loyalty, compassion and self-sacrifice. He also believes that some satisfactions in life can only be won through sheer hard work. But he is not remotely interested in *preaching* to young readers through his stories – his concern is to write the best story he can. Since he respects qualities like loyalty, compassion and putting other people before yourself, characters who live by such values are often at the centre of his stories.

His beliefs are not based on any one religion. Much of the art, music, literature and architecture which gives him satisfaction derives from the world's great religions and for that, he is grateful. Most of those religions, he believes, share common values about the importance of families, how we treat each other and how we treat the world around us. 'There is 95 per cent agreement between the faiths but, to my mind, it is the 5 per cent which divides us.' For him, Jesus is one of the greatest of moral teachers and the Bible a treasure hoard of some of the most powerful stories in the world, which have been the basis of the law and morality by which we live. But while Jesus is centrally important to him, the Church is not. He can't believe some of the teaching about heaven and hell and the afterlife. He dislikes the rigid beliefs and rules of some of those – Christians and believers in other faiths – who practise their religion over-zealously with little tolerance for the views of others. Such rigidity, in his view, has often distanced them from the great mass of men and women and that, he believes, is very dangerous.

Michael as Writer in Residence at Tate Britain, 2000.

What Next?

Michael does not think he will ever give up telling stories through his novels. He never seems to run out of ideas. For example, he hasn't yet written a story about elephants, though he has always wanted to – they're his favourite animals. He'll always be looking for the next challenge.

He has written the words for a couple of operas – that avenue could be worth exploring further. He's got more to learn about scripts for films and plays. Above all, though, he would like to write the kind of poems that would lead him into a new kind of writing altogether. He admires poets who are able, like Charles Causley, to extract the essence from a story and tell it in very few words in verse. That's something he doesn't think he can yet do.

If he could, he'd turn himself into a combination of his two great writer-heroes – 'my champions', he calls them: Robert Louis Stevenson and Ted Hughes. Both wrote poetry, both wrote novels. Both wrote for children and for grown-ups – he'd like to write a book like *Treasure Island* which you can read when you're ten, or twenty, or sixty, enjoying it for different reasons each time. 'I'd be happy', says Michael, 'if I could write with the power of Ted Hughes and the narrative skill of Robert Louis Stevenson.'

He'd also like to think that what he writes would help to bring stories, poems and plays more into the centre of British life. Other countries value their writers far more than we do. In France, for example, every town seems to have squares and streets named in honour of writers – 'Place Victor Hugo' or 'Rue Balzac'. When Michael and Clare were being driven around Dublin by their friend, the poet Seamus Heaney, they pulled up to ask for help from a policeman. Before they could speak, the policeman smiled: 'Ah, Seamus, is it you, for heavens' sakes! And how are you today?' Everyone in Dublin seemed to know him! In Britain, Michael says, 'We have writers who are famous all over the world, but we don't do enough to honour or celebrate them publicly at home.'

Whether his future work is inside the covers of a book, on the stage or on the screen, Michael will surely continue to write about ideas, people and places which excite, amuse or upset him.

A young fan in Scotland summed things up neatly. He had been very excited by reading *Cool!*. Now he wanted to know more about his new favourite author when he met Lindsey Fraser, the organiser of Michael's Children's Laureate programme:

'Is he big?'

'Well, big-ish – he's not that big', said Lindsey, rather puzzled.

'He should be big. He writes big stories.'

'Not really, you know. Quite a lot of his books are short-ish.'

'No, I don't mean that. The stories are big. He writes about big things.'

'Yes, I suppose he does.'

'You see, when I read them, *I feel big*.'

'That'll do', thinks Michael.

Michael rowing his boat.

The Story That Wrote Itself

The Story That Wrote Itself
by Michael Morpurgo

I have to find quiet places to write. I don't like noise around me when I'm trying to weave a story inside my head. That's why I went to Samson Island in the first place, to write a story. But then it wrote itself.

*　　*　　*

The lady at the bed and breakfast where I was staying on Bryher Island said it would be just the place I was looking for to write my story. A deserted island called Samson, a few rabbits and some terns for company – a perfect place, she said. What more could I want? It was a fine summer's day, flat calm sea, cloudless blue sky. She made me a picnic, a ham roll, some crisps, an apple and a can of lager. She lent me her boat too. So that morning, I rowed myself across to Samson – it was only a mile or so, an easy row. Samson is a small

241

green island, just two hills covered in bracken, a spit of low scrubby land in between, white sandy beaches on one side, cliffs and rocks on the other. As I looked over my shoulder at the island it somehow seemed as if it knew I was coming, as if it was waiting to make me welcome.

I hauled my boat up onto the beach and threw out the anchor. Then I found myself a place in the dunes to sit and write. I opened my writing book and stared down at the empty pages. But the ideas didn't come and the pages stayed obstinately empty. For an hour or so I doodled a rabbit, doodled a gull, doodled a boat and, gazing idly around me, chewed on my pencil. That was when I noticed the narrow peaty black track winding its way up the hillside through the bracken. I made up my mind. I would give up my story and go exploring instead. So I left the dunes and followed wherever the track might lead me.

The bracken was head high on either side, and I could see now what had made the track. Rabbits – they'd left their little brown droppings everywhere. All at once I came upon a ruined cottage. Little remained, only the stone walls and a chimney. No windows, no doors. I went in. There was an old stone fireplace at one end, and on the ground I noticed a broken clay pipe and some limpet shells scattered, which was strange because the cottage was a long way from the shore. I wondered then if this was the only cottage on the island. I followed more peaty black tracks and discovered a dozen others, all of them in ruins, some more ruined than others. I found a well, too, in the middle of the island, but it was dry.

I ate my picnic in glorious sunshine, sitting in the middle of the highest cottage on the island, and, as I ate, I spread out all the treasures I had found that morning. There was the clay pipe, a sole of a shoe, and, best of all, a bent copper penny dated 1881. I was thirsty so I drank my can of lager. Perhaps it was the sunshine, perhaps it was the lager, perhaps it was the long walk over the island, but suddenly I felt very tired. I took one look at the empty pages of my writing book and decided the story could wait. I wanted to sleep. I took off my shirt, lay down in the sun in the roofless cottage and was asleep before I knew it.

I was woken by the sound of the wind whistling about the chimney of the cottage. I had no idea how long I had been asleep, but it must have been some time, because the world about me had changed utterly. The blue sky was gone. Great grey clouds were rolling in, and, as I got to my feet and pulled on my shirt, I felt the first heavy drops of rain. I looked out to sea. It was choppy – I would have a hard row back. I gathered up my treasures and as fast as I could I made my way back down the hill, past the well, down towards the beach where I'd left the boat. But the beach was empty. In fact the beach was hardly there at all. The tide had come right in and covered it almost completely. The boat had gone. I raced across the island, clambered over the rocks, splashed through rockpools, all the while hoping that I would find it washed up somewhere. It was nowhere.

By now the storm was whipping itself into a rage, the rain and wind stinging my face as I ran. I had to do something. I tried shouting. I tried waving, but I knew it was hopeless. No one would hear me, not in this wind. There were no boats out on the water and even if there had been, no one could have seen me through the driving rain. There was only one thing for it. I would have to find shelter and just wait for someone to come and find me. I thought then of the cottage where I had eaten my picnic and slept away my afternoon, and remembered the old stone fire-place and the chimney above it which had fallen in and made a tumble-down roof. I remembered noticing

there was dry bracken in the fireplace, as if someone before me had used it as a bed.

It was a long walk up the hill again, but it was worth it when I got there. The bracken was still dry. The roof of fallen chimney stones made a perfect shelter against wind and rain. I was chilled to the bone. I took off everything that was wet and crawled in under the bracken. It was prickly and dusty, but it was a lot better than freezing to death. I scavenged the last crumbs of my sandwich, licked my crisp packet clean, ate my apple core and drained the dregs of my can of lager. It wasn't much but it was something. I wasn't that unhappy either. I was safe enough. All I had to do was to wait out the storm and someone would come and fetch me. I would be fine – or so I told myself.

But as it got darker my fragile confidence soon drained away. Before long it was so black about me that I could hardly see the wall of the cottage. Sleep would be best, I thought. Time passes quickly when you're asleep. I closed my eyes, but sleep wouldn't come.

Then I heard rustling outside the walls of the cottage. 'Anyone there?' I called out. No-one replied. Perhaps it's rabbits, I thought. Then the rustling came closer, louder. 'Big rabbits', I said out loud, trying to laugh it off, trying to cheer myself up. That was the moment I looked up at the gaping black windows and felt eyes staring back at me. Something or someone was out there, I was sure of it now. I squeezed my eyes tight shut, gritted my teeth, trying to control my rising terror.

When I opened my eyes he was sitting there opposite me on the bracken, a young boy in shirt and breeches, his knees drawn up under his chin. He was studying me closely. 'You're in our cottage', the boy said. 'It weren't always like this you know. It was the Frenchie ship that did for us. We was all right before that – enough to eat, just about – limpets, always limpets of course, and potatoes, fish when we could catch 'em off the rocks. Water in the well. We was all right. Then one morning there was this ship, washed up on the beach, she was – our beach. Anything we find on our island is ours – driftwood for winter fires,

clothes from drowned sailors. So, happy as larks we all ran down to the beach. There was a few frenchies on board, but they was too weak to fight us. We put 'em down in the hold and then we were all there up on deck trying to decide what to do.'

'My pa's idea it was. "What do we want with a great big ship?" he says. "Let's sell it to the Navy, get some money, put new rooves on our houses maybe and buy a couple of fishing boats so's we can go out fishing again. This ship could be the best thing that's ever happened to us. We'll see how she floats on the next tide. If she's sound we'll take her to Penzance and sell her."'

'No-one argued. Everyone was too happy to argue. We couldn't believe our luck. That night we all had a

bit of a party, Grandpa Zac on the squeezeybox and everyone dancing and singing. Even Grandma Beth had a dance.'

'The next morning I was there to wave them off, along with all the others they left behind. We stood there watching the sails 'til we couldn't see them any more. My Ma and Pa, my big brother Jim and Grandpa Zac, they were all on that ship. They needed all the hands they could get. I wanted to go, but I was too little. They left all the little ones and the old ones behind, except Grandpa Zac because he was a good navigator. Been all over the world he had.'

The boy's eyes never left me for a moment, and mine never left him. I tried to convince myself that it was a dream I was in. I tried to wake up from it, but I couldn't. This was no dream. It was real.

'You know what happened?' I saw he was crying now, brushing away his tears with the back of his hand. 'You know what happened? They never got to Penzance, none of them. The ship went down on the Wolf Rock. They found bits and pieces of it washed up on the mainland. Everyone on board was drowned, all of them, every single one of them. Back here on Samson, only Grandma Beth wanted to stay. The others said the place was cursed and left. So we were alone here on Samson, just Grandma Beth and me. She refused to leave because she knew Grandpa Zac's ghost still lived on the island and she wasn't going to leave him, curse or no curse. Then I got sick. I woke up one night with pains in my ears so bad I thought I'd die. In the morning Grandma Beth went to fetch water to clean me up, but the well was dry. You can't live without water, can you? So she lit a beacon and they came and fetched us off. We went to live on Bryher. That's where she died.'

'And I grew up deaf as a post. Never heard the sea, nor the birds, nor a human voice ever again. They called me the Birdman because I fed the birds and talked to them, and they liked me and came around me. Then I died, but I come back here whenever I feel like it, we all do. It's still our place. We're still here. Always will be. You can sleep in our cottage, I don't mind. Sleep well.' And he was gone, just like that.

I did sleep, and when I woke I still remembered the

boy. That's why I knew he was not a dream. I never remember my dreams. Anyway, to cut a long story short, they came for me early the next morning when the wind had died down and brought me back here to Bryher. I lay in a wonderfully hot bath and shivered the cold out of me. At breakfast, I apologised again to the lady about her boat, but apparently someone had just telephoned her to say it had been found washed-up in Popplestones Bay on Bryher. No damage, just one oar and an anchor missing. 'Besides', the lady went on, 'If anything, it's me should be saying sorry to you. After all, I was the one who suggested you went to Samson, wasn't I? What a horrible night you must have had.' As she poured my tea she bent over me and chuckled. 'They say Samson is haunted, you know. I don't believe it, of course. Don't believe in ghosts. Well, at least you'll have a great story to write won't you? My Night on Haunted Island. How's that for a good title?'

'Not bad', I replied, 'but I think I've got a better one: The Story That Wrote Itself.'

* * *

It wrote itself that same afternoon. I hope you've enjoyed it.

About the Author

Geoff Fox taught in schools before he joined the School of Education at Exeter University, where he worked in the English and drama department for many years. He has been a frequent contributor to workshops and conferences in the United Kingdom and abroad and has also visited numerous countries, from Brazil to Outer Mongolia, to work with children, undergraduates and teachers. He has written and reviewed extensively, chiefly about the teaching of literature, children's books and drama. He was a founding editor in 1970 of the international quarterly, *Children's Literature in Education*, which he continues to edit. In retirement from the university, he spends some of his time storytelling in schools, taking odd jobs as an actor, helping to run the Crediton Arts Centre and writing, including one or two forays into fiction and drama.

Acknowledgements

I would like to thank those whose support has been invaluable during the preparation of this book. Some had little choice in listening to me thinking aloud as the manuscript developed, demonstrating more patience than they probably felt; a number of them read sections of the manuscript. Clare Dowdall of the University of Plymouth, Peter Hamilton of the Crediton Arts Centre and Mary Pereira of Hayward's School, Crediton, gave valuable advice in the early stages. Pupils from Hayward's, Morpurgo enthusiasts all, read extracts from my manuscript and offered frank and mostly supportive comments. James Walker gave me insights into his meticulous preparations for the role of the Birdman in Theatre Alibi's production of *Why the Whales Came.* Jamie Stuart, landlord of the Duke of York at Iddesleigh, provided sustaining hospitality during some lengthy tape recording sessions. For the publishers, Kate Agnew and Simon Flynn have always been tactfully perceptive in their swift responses to work in progress.

I would like to thank Pam Barnard, who made notes through hours of interviews and has listened, read, commented and encouraged beyond any reasonable expectation. I am particularly grateful to Clare and Michael Morpurgo for their close involvement in the whole project. Despite all the demands upon them during Michael's time as Laureate, they have been unstinting in the gifts of their time, interest and support.

GF

The Publishers would like to thank Michael Morpurgo for his support and enthusiasm and for his invaluable help in the writing of this book. Our thanks also go to Clare Morpurgo who provided the family photographs and was endlessly patient with our queries and to Michael Foreman for all his help with the illustrations.